PAINTING MARITIME LANDSCAPES

JOHN C. PELLEW, N. A., A. W. S.

PAINTING MARITIME LANDSCAPES

WATSON-GUPTILL PUBLICATIONS/NEW YORK

PITMAN PUBLISHING/LONDON

First published 1973 in the United States and Canada by Watson-Guptill Publications,
a division of Billboard Publications, Inc.
One Astor Plaza, New York, N.Y. 10036

Published simultaneously in Great Britain by Sir Isaac Pitman & Sons Ltd.,
39 Parker Street, Kingsway, London WC2B 5PB
U.K. ISBN 0-273-00409-3

Manufactured in Japan

Library of Congress Cataloging in Publication Data
Pellew, John C. 1903–
    Painting maritime landscapes.
    SUMMARY: Basic techniques for capturing the primary
elements of the sea in oil, acrylic, and watercolor.
    Bibliography: p.
    1. Marine painting—Technique—Juvenile literature.
[1. Marine painting—Technique] I. Title.
ND1370.P44   751.4   73-5688
ISBN 0-8230-3695-2

First Printing, 1973

Edited by Lois Miller
Designed by James Craig and Robert Fillie
Set in 10 point Medallion by Publishers Graphics, Inc.
Printed and bound in Japan by Toppan Printing Company Ltd.

This one is for Jamie

Himself and Herself—the Two Pellews (Statuettes by Don Carlon)

Acknowledgments

I especially wish to thank Don Holden, Watson-Guptill Editorial Director, for his help and encouragement, and Lois Miller, my editor, for making my shaky prose shape up. Thanks also to Diane Casella Hines for many valuable suggestions and to my wife Elsie for the many tedious hours spent typing. And thanks to my friend John Pike, who first suggested that I write a book on painting.

Contents

Introduction

This is a book for the artist who's especially fond of the subject matter found along the shore, the artist who likes to walk the beaches after a September gale or climb ledges slippery with rockweed and rough with barnacles, who finds a whole new world in the magic of a pool left behind by the outgoing tide, who's never lost interest in or failed to be thrilled by the armies of dark, pointed firs that march down to the sea on the Maine headlands. It's a book for the many students who have worked with me in Maine and on Cape Ann. And it's also for Irene, who desperately wanted to know how to paint rocks under water.

So much about whom this book is for—now, what's it about? Many things, but mainly it's about the problems an artist faces when painting coastal subject matter. I don't want to set down formulas for painting this or that subject, but I hope I can act as a guide, so that the business of painting outdoors won't be as bewildering to you as it often seems to the student or amateur painter. There are often simple solutions to problems that seem quite difficult to the inexperienced. This won't exactly be a how-to-do-it book, but rather one that will tell you how an experienced painter has worked out a lot of the technical problems found in painting the coast in New England and elsewhere.

There are painters who make painting the desert their life's work, and I'm sure they do so because they love doing it. I've painted in many parts of the world, but I must confess that although I've found beauty in places far from the ocean, I'm never completely satisfied when I'm working away from the coast. And that's strange, because I've never thought of myself as a marine painter, a specialist in rocks and pounding surf.

Perhaps I like the coast because I've lived most of my life beside or close to the sea. My earliest memories are of great southwesterly gales that brought tremendous seas into Mount's Bay in Cornwall, England, and of waking in the night to hear rockets summon a volunteer lifeboat crew to the aid of a ship in trouble off the shore or perhaps wrecked beneath the awesome cliffs at Land's End. Even now, after almost fifty years, I can close my eyes and see the fishing fleet, with its burnt sienna sails, putting out on a summer evening from Newlyn across the bay.

Since that time, I've lived on Long Island and in New England. I've painted up and down the coast in all seasons, finding subject matter everywhere. So, I'll put it this way—I enjoy painting anywhere, but I truly feel at home when I'm painting the maritime subjects I've lived with most of my life.

A Bright Day. Watercolor on illustration board, 7½″ x 11″. I painted this picture on Good Harbor Beach, Gloucester, on a bright September day. This little watercolor is an eighth-sheet—that is, one part of a regular 22″ x 30″ sheet cut into eight parts. It's a good size for small, quick sketches. I haven't seen many amateur artists doing "quickies." I think they're too anxious to take home large pictures. Some of the best watercolors ever painted were done on this size paper. You can learn a lot about watercolor techniques by doing them. You won't be so afraid of spoiling the painting, and your coverage will result in a more spontaneous effect. Then, too, it takes less time to paint such a small picture. The inexperienced painter always spends too much time on half-sheet paintings. The eighth-sheet quickie is a great aid in overcoming the slow-motion approach to outdoor watercolor sketching.

1 *Materials and Equipment*

Working in three mediums—oil, acrylic, and watercolor—as I do, I'm often asked which I like best. My answer is always the same. I like all three. I think the specialist in one medium misses half the fun of being an artist. Most of the truly great painters worked in both oil and watercolor. Some, Degas and Daumier, for example, even modeled in wax.

Characteristics of Paint

Today, we think of oil paint as an opaque medium, of watercolor as transparent. Acrylic can be either opaque or transparent. Let's compare them.

Oil. Many painters, including me, find something extremely satisfying in the rich, fat, sticky qualities of oil paint. This is especially true when certain mediums and varnishes are used with the paint. (I'll comment on these later.) There's a tacky quality that's a distinctive feature of slow-drying oil paint. Because of its slow-drying nature, oil allows us to use certain types of brushwork that aren't possible with fast-drying acrylic and, of course, are absolutely impossible (as well as undesirable) with transparent watercolor. Glazing and the half-covering scumbling technique, which involves dragging a brush loaded with paint over a partially dry undertone, create textures difficult to imitate with any other medium.

Acrylic. When used in an opaque fashion, acrylic paint has much the same appearance as oil paint. In fact, when acrylic is varnished, it's often difficult to distinguish it from oil paint. Acrylic paint also yields interesting results when used in transparent washes on watercolor paper. Because it's fast-drying, you can use one acrylic wash over another without disturbing the first one. For this reason, watercolor painters should try experimenting with acrylic. However, I don't think the popular acrylic paints should be used as a substitute for any other medium. I like them for their own particular qualities, not because I can imitate the effects of another medium with them.

Watercolor. Of course, watercolor paint has nothing in common with oil paint. It's foolish to try to make a watercolor painting look like an oil. But in spite of this, some of the watercolors that show up in exhibitions are heavily opaque in treatment, and some are even varnished. I don't understand the thinking of the painters who produce them. Surely, there's nothing quite as lovely as a well-executed transparent watercolor painting on good quality paper.

Palette

I've said it before and I'll say it again—the amateur painter loads his paintbox with too many tubes of color! The following are the only colors I carry for oil, acrylic, and watercolor.

Oil. Here's my landscape sketching palette for oil paint: titanium white, cadmium yellow light, yellow ochre, raw sienna, cadmium orange, cadmium red light, burnt sienna, burnt umber, cerulean blue, and Thalo (phthalocyanine) blue. I don't carry any prepared greens. I like to mix my greens from various combinations of the yellows and blues I carry. (I'll discuss the characteristics of these colors in more detail in *Color Characteristics and Color Mixing*, page 25.)

Acrylic. My acrylic palette varies only slightly from my oil palette: titanium white, Hansa yellow, yellow ochre, raw sienna, cadmium red light, burnt sienna, burnt umber, cerulean blue, Thalo blue, and black. My only bright acrylic yellow is Hansa, which replaces the cadmium yellow I use in oil and is said to be more permanent. I've yet to find a good alizarin crimson in acrylic. However, I occasionally use the new Naphtol crimson when I need cooler reds and violets.

Watercolor. Here's a list of what I'm presently using in my watercolor palette: cadmium yellow light, gamboge, yellow ochre, raw sienna, cadmium red light, alizarin crimson, burnt sienna, burnt umber, cerulean blue, Thalo blue, and ivory black. Instead of cadmium red, I substitute Winsor & Newton's cadmium scarlet when I can get it. Cadmium yellow is quite opaque, so I use gamboge when I want a transparent wash. I use the ivory black only to tone down and take the "sting" out of an intense color such as Thalo blue. If you must have a watercolor green, try Thalo.

Brushes and Knives

Now for a few words on the tools of the trade, starting with brushes and knives.

Oil. I use two types of brushes with oil paint—brights and flats. Brights are rather square with short bristles. Flats are thicker with longer bristles or hairs. Round bristle brushes are also available, but I've never found them very useful for landscape work. I prefer brights. They're just right for working with plenty of thick, juicy oil paint. The flats are too long and pliable for my taste. For work on 12″ x 16″ panels, I carry one Number 10 and two each of Numbers 2, 3, and 7. These, along with a small pointed sable for an occasional fine line, are all the oil brushes you'll need. The flat red sables made for oil painting are best suited to smooth, detailed work done in the studio, not on location. Your paintbox for oil paint should also contain two knives—a palette knife and a painting knife (Figure 1). Use the larger one, the palette knife, to scrape paint from your palette and canvas. The smaller, pointed painting knife is the one to use for painting.

Acrylic. You can use the same brushes and knives for acrylic painting that you use for oil. Some artists prefer the newer nylon brushes. I know they can be washed out easily, but I like the "feel" of the oil painter's brights. I don't recommend using sable brushes for acrylic painting either. Accidents can happen. A bristle brush can be replaced cheaply, but sable brushes are expensive. When you're working with acrylic, remember to keep your brushes wet. Don't lay aside a brush with paint in it even for a few minutes. The paint on the brush will dry rapidly and the brush may be ruined forever. Drop your used acrylic brushes into a container of water as soon as you're finished with them. And wash them out with soap and warm water as soon as your day's work is done.

Watercolor. The best brushes for watercolor, of course, are sables. No other brushes intended for use with watercolor hive the snap and spring of sables. Four or five of them are all you really need. Most of the time, I get along very well with four—a 1″ flat, a Number 9 round, a Number 7 round, and a small Number 2 for fine

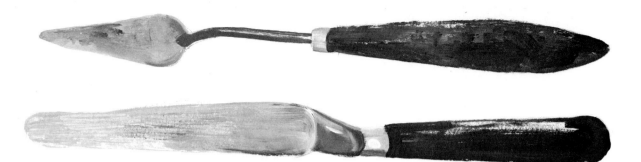

Figure 1. These two knives are useful for oil painting. The palette knife (bottom) is used to scrape paint from your canvas or palette. The painting knife (top) is the one you apply the paint with.

lines. I rinse these out in clear water and use soap on them only about once a year. I know of painters who use the cheaper oxhair brushes for watercolor. These aren't bad, but if you can afford the more expensive sables, buy them.

Painting Surfaces

Now let's consider what you should paint on. There are many painting surfaces to choose from, and you should be aware of which surfaces are best suited to each medium.

Oil. You can paint with oil on Masonite, Upson board, canvas, and even on paper. Masonite and Upson board are hardboards you can buy at lumberyards and building supply houses. They come in large 4′ x 8′ sheets and have to be cut to size. This is no problem for the handyman, but some ladies might find it difficult.

Masonite is a fine, rigid support. I find the ⅛″ thickness good for pictures up to 16″ x 20″—larger than that, I prefer to use canvas. Masonite is probably the most permanent painting support ever discovered, especially when it's primed on both sides and around the edges.

Upson is a wallboard 3/16″ thick. It's something like heavy cardboard, smooth on one side with a canvas-like texture on the other. If you're painting for posterity, you've no guarantee that Upson board is permanent. But it's fine for sketches, especially the outdoor kind. And if by chance you do paint a masterpiece on it, the museums will take care of it—so don't worry.

It's best to use canvas for large oil paintings, and some painters like the springy feel of a well-stretched canvas even in the smaller sizes. You can purchase linen and cotton canvas ready-primed by the yard or roll. If you want to go to a little trouble—and incidentally save a little money—you can prepare it yourself. I'll tell you how later on in this chapter.

There's also something to be said for oil painting on watercolor paper. The 19th-century English landscape painter John Constable often sketched with oil on paper. The Victoria and Albert Museum in London has a large collection of his sketches. I'm sure the paper he used must have been high-quality watercolor paper. Most of his small, charming impressions of nature are as fresh and luminous today as they were the day he painted them, a hundred years ago.

I've used watercolor paper for oil painting without preparing it in any way

Beached Boat. Acrylic on cardboard, 8″ x 11″. This is a small, quick acrylic sketch I painted on a piece of ordinary cardboard to demonstrate the use of acrylic paints to an outdoor class. I first coated the cardboard with white latex house paint, then mixed a little powdered raw umber pigment with the white latex and overpainted a gray tone. This is an inexpensive way to make sketching panels. They're not permanent, but they're good for experimenting and demonstrating techniques—for bold, broad statements, which is what outdoor impressions should be.

and it has worked fine. It's a bit too absorbent, but I don't mind that. If you want a less absorbent surface, you can size the paper with acrylic gesso that has been thinned to a consistency somewhat thinner than milk. When painting on paper, you must secure the paper to a rigid support. I use a Masonite panel slightly larger than the paper I work on. I simply fasten the paper to the panel with a piece of masking tape across each corner.

Acrylic. Many painters use the wrong painting surfaces for acrylic. Just the other day, I found four of my students gayly slapping acrylic on ready-made canvas panels. When questioned, they told me that their artist's supply dealer had said the panels were suitable for both oil and acrylic. "But there ain't no such animal!" Unless you have proof that a panel was prepared only with acrylic gesso, don't take a chance on it. With the least bit of oil in the priming of such a panel, there's a good chance that the acrylic will crack or peel with age.

The acrylic surface you use should be fairly absorbent. The 300 lb. watercolor paper is an excellent painting surface for acrylic. Raw linen stretched and primed with acrylic gesso is also a good surface. And there's nothing wrong with plain old cardboard, either, if it's fairly thick and sturdy. A bit further on, I'll tell you how to prepare it.

Watercolor. There's no substitute for high-quality, handmade watercolor paper. The 300 lb. paper is the best weight to use. It costs more than the lighter weight papers (70 and 140 lb.), but it's worth it. There's no need to stretch it and it doesn't buckle. The 140 lb. paper is good for working on location, if you stick to the smaller sizes—quarter sheet, for instance. If you use 140 lb. paper in larger sizes, you should stretch it first by wetting it, laying it flat on your drawing board, and taping the edges down to the board with gummed paper tape such as the kind used for packages.

Watercolor paper is available in three surface textures—hot-pressed, or smooth, cold-pressed, or medium-rough, and rough. The medium-rough texture of cold-pressed paper is most useful in watercolor landscape painting. The really rough-surfaced paper is actually too rough for small pictures. Recently, painters have also been experimenting with very smooth hot-pressed paper. I used it myself for some of the paintings reproduced in this book (the captions identify them), and I'm beginning to like it very much. Washes dry rapidly on smooth-surfaced paper because there isn't much grain for them to sink into. It's also easy to sponge out lights, scrape with a knife, and scratch out with a fingernail on the hard, smooth surface.

If you're accustomed to painting on rougher watercolor papers, you may be discouraged by your first attempts on smooth paper. However, after a few tries you'll see certain interesting things begin to happen that aren't possible on the usual rough-surfaced paper.

The smooth papers were originally used for commercial work and can be found in artist's supply stores under such names as illustration board, kidd finish, Bristol board and plate finish.

Preparing Canvas

I prepare my canvas for oil painting in the following manner. I stretch raw Belgian linen on regular wooden canvas stretcher strips. Then I spread acrylic gesso (well-stirred in the can) on the canvas and press it into the surface with a wide putty knife. When this is dry I paint on a second coat with a 3" house painter's brush.

Whether or not it's good practice to paint with oil over acrylic priming is still being debated. I've done it for years and find no signs of cracking or peeling in any of my paintings. In Wendon Blake's *Complete Guide to Acrylic Painting*, there's a description of how to prepare an acrylic underpainting for use with oil paint. I've done this many times with good results and my oil paintings haven't shown any change in the past six or seven years. However, Ralph Mayer, Technical Editor of *American Artist*, says, "I don't advise combining acrylic products with oil paint in any way." So there you are. You'll have to decide for yourself. I can only repeat that personally I've found acrylic gesso to be an excellent ground for oil paint.

Preparing Masonite Panels

I paint most of my smaller oils on panels of untempered Masonite and Upson board. I prepare both these surfaces in the same manner. I lightly sand the smooth side (the side that you'll paint on), of the Masonite with fine sandpaper so that the gesso will adhere to it more readily. (Sanding isn't necessary with Upson board, which already has a somewhat rough surface.) After I wipe off the dust with a damp cloth, I give the surface a coat of acrylic gesso, using a 2″ nylon house painter's brush. When it's dry, I turn the panel over and give the back a coat. This is the only coat the back of the panel receives. How many coats you put on the front is up to you. I usually thin the gesso with a little water and apply three coats. I also paint the edges of the panel with the gesso. This completely seals the panel, giving the surface greater permanence. You can also apply gesso to the panel with a roller.

Cardboard

There's nothing wrong with a nice, heavy piece of cardboard for sketching with either oil or acrylic. It's not going to last forever, of course, but it will last a long time if it's properly prepared. The kind of cardboard the dealer calls chipboard is the best. It's sold in sheets measuring 30″ x 40″ and is like the cardboard used for the backs of paper pads, but thicker. You can coat it with acrylic gesso on both sides, just as with Masonite and Upson board.

However, first try this. Get a small bottle of white shellac and some denatured alcohol. Cut the shellac with the alcohol until it runs like water. Test the mixture before you use it. If it dries with a gloss, add more alcohol. Paint both sides of the cardboard with the diluted shellac. The chipboard is gray in color and, therefore, you'll have a pre-toned panel. Remember, I said that cardboard is fine for *sketching*. These panels are cheap, handy, and easy to prepare—but don't do paintings on them that you want your great, great-grandchildren to admire.

Easels

An easel that's to be used in the field should be sturdy, easy to set up and take down, not apt to blow over in a breeze, and—most important—not too heavy to carry. Easels used outdoors are called sketching easels, and along with paintboxes, they're necessary requirements for outdoor painting. So let's take a look at what's available.

Upright. In outdoor painting, it's often necessary to stand in the sun. I find it very difficult to judge tonal values with the sun shining directly down on my painting surface, as it does when the surface is placed in a horizontal position. The sun produces an extremely bright glare particularly on white watercolor paper. When I work on an upright easel, I can always turn the easel so that the paper, canvas, or panel is shaded. Also, I do a lot of outdoor painting demonstrations for workshop classes. In order for 25 or 30 people at a time to see what I'm doing, it's necessary that the painting surface be upright.

My choice for all upright work is the old-time Anderson, or Gloucester, easel (Figure 2). It's a sturdy wooden easel, light enough to carry yet heavy enough not to blow over. (Most of the lightweight metal easels are too light—and that's exactly why they blow over and are easily damaged.) The Gloucester easel has no wing nuts or bolts to fool with or lose, and its legs are self-locking and spread wide—a good feature when the wind is blowing. It will hold anything from a small panel to a 25″ x 30″ canvas. It isn't easy to find this easel in artist's supply stores anymore, but they're still made by H. A. Coon, 7 Highland Court, Gloucester, Massachusetts 01930.

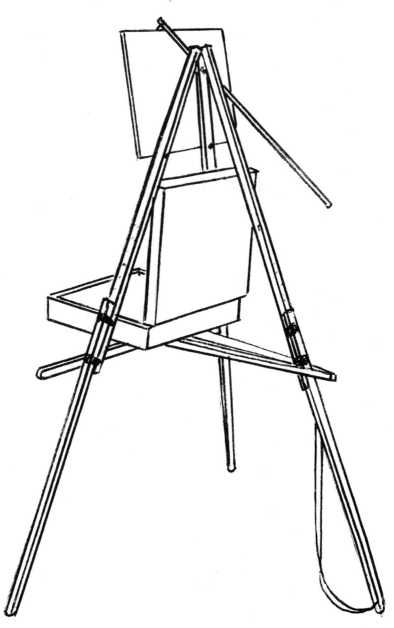

Figure 2. This is the Anderson, or Gloucester, easel. It's a sturdy wooden easel that conveniently holds my paper, canvas, or panel, as well as my paintbox.

Watercolor. As I said, I use the same upright easel for all my outdoor painting, including watercolor. But many watercolorists do without an easel altogether. They simply squat on the ground and prop the drawing board—with the watercolor paper pinned to it—against a rock or anything else that happens to be handy.

Most watercolor painters favor an easel made especially for watercolor painting. It has a platform that can be tilted from a horizontal to a vertical position, which holds the drawing board at any angle. This easel is a bit heavy, but it's probably the best for watercolor painting.

Combinations. The so-called French combination easel and paintbox is also quite popular, but I find it too heavy to carry around. This outfit is good-looking and well-made, but the business of setting it up and taking it down is just too complicated for me.

Paintboxes

There are a variety of paintboxes on the market. Some are made of wood, some of metal. Forget the metal ones. They rattle like the devil and it's easy to dent them. A few dents in the right places and the lid refuses to close, or worse yet, won't open at all! For outdoor work in oil or acrylic, the standard 12″ x 16″ wooden box fills the bill quite well. Slots in the lid hold a 12″ x 16″ panel, and a wooden palette of the same size comes with the box. Some painters like the 16″ x 20″ size, but I think that a 12″ x 16″ panel is the ideal size for sketching from nature. Although the panel has to be 16″ wide to fit into the slots in the lid, it can be less than 12″ high. You can use a 10″ x 16″ if you wish. For acrylic work, I use a 12″ x 16″ piece of white Formica in place of the wooden palette that comes with the box.

A poet once asked, "What is so rare as a day in June?" I'd answer, "a good watercolor box!" I carry my tubes of paint in an old tobacco tin. I also have a rather beat-up palette box that has compartments for ten tubes. The lid of the box flips open to form a palette. The bottom of the box has a thumbhole, and I can hold the whole thing in my left hand. Students constantly ask me where I got this box. Sad to say, it can no longer be found anywhere—they're no longer manufactured. However, there's a paintbox on the market with a sliding cover that opens into a palette. It's made of a heavy-weight metal, much better than some of those lightweight aluminum things. When I use it, I just take out the palette and leave the box at home. I don't need all that room for my few tubes of paint.

Mediums

First of all, what is a medium? A medium is a liquid or jelly-like substance used for thinning paints during the process of painting. Of course, the medium used to thin watercolor is water. Having disposed of that, I'll go on to the more complex mediums used with oil and acrylic.

Ready-mixed oil. There are a number of mediums for oil paint on the market, but I can recommend only a couple. One is Copal Painting Medium made by Grumbacher, the other is Weber's Res-n-Gel. The first contains Congo copal resin, linseed oil, and stand oil. It imparts a nice satiny gloss to oil paint, dries well, and even smells good. It comes with the blessing of Frederic Taubes, who has written several books on painting techniques. However, Max Doerner and Ralph Mayer, also experts, advise the artist to avoid using anything that contains copal. So what's the poor painter to do? I've used Copal Painting Medium for several years and nothing has happened to my paintings yet. Guess I'll uncross my fingers.

Willi Painting. Oil on cardboard, 9″ x 12″. Since I often travel with a group of students, it's not surprising that they appear from time to time in my paintings. However, it's no problem to find and paint other artists at work on the Maine coast in the summer or fall. This tall girl was so absorbed in her painting that she never suspected I was putting her in my sketchbook. I've never seen anyone place a canvas as high on the easel as this young lady did. I don't like to reach that far up when I'm painting, but she seemed to be doing all right. The foliage, trees, bushes, and grass had all turned to autumn colors and were complemented nicely by a small triangle of blue ocean coming in at the left. The dusty road leads to Hendrick's Head Light.

I include Res-n-Gel when I travel because it comes in a tube and there's no bottle of sticky liquid to break or leak. Mixing a little gel with each mound of paint on my palette shortens the drying time and imparts a nice buttery consistency to the paint. It's great for outdoor work.

Mixing your own. Perhaps the best way to find a painting medium that really suits you is to mix it yourself. It's not difficult to do. There are several formulas in the handbooks of both Ralph Mayer and Fred Taubes (see the bibliography in the back of this book). Renoir used a mixture of 1 part linseed oil to 1 part turpentine. Now that's easy—and safe.

A medium I've been using in the studio recently is composed of 1 part linseed oil, 1 part Venice turpentine, and 2 parts turpentine. I put these all together in a bottle and shake them. Venice turpentine is the exudation from the Austrian larch (a tree in the pine family). It's heavy, thick, and difficult to pour. I make it more fluid by standing the bottle in the sun for a couple of hours to warm it up. You can also put the bottle in hot, not boiling, water. Venice turpentine can be purchased in 2 oz. bottles or larger cans in art supply stores. Whenever I mention turpentine, I mean pure *gum* turpentine. Be sure the word gum is on the label if you buy your "turps" in gallon cans at the local paint or hardware store as I do.

Another medium I've used contains sun-thickened linseed oil. This medium is a favorite with many because sun-thickened oil is a rapid drier. Here's the formula: 4 parts damar varnish, 2 parts sun-thickened linseed oil, 1 part Venice turpentine, and 4 parts gum turpentine. I took this formula from *The Artist's Handbook of Materials and Techniques,* by Ralph Mayer.

All the mediums I mention here give oil paint more or less of an enamel-like quality and a satiny gloss, depending on how much you mix into the paint. I suggest you get along with as little medium as possible, because the paint manufacturer has already loaded his paint with medium or binding materials. You can get rid of some of these oils by setting your paint out on bond paper and letting it dry for a while before you place it on your palette.

These rich, fatty mediums are best for studio work, where finish and detail are desired. For direct or alla prima painting on location, it's best to stay with the handy tube of Res-n-Gel or the half-oil, half-turpentine mixture.

Acrylic. Mediums for acrylic are simpler than those for oil—at least for me. I use only water when I paint on location with acrylic. There's already enough medium in the paint. Any addition only increases its drying time, and I want my acrylic to dry fast—that's the advantage of using it.

There are two acrylic mediums—glossy and matte. When you use the glossy medium with acrylic, the picture dries with a shine. If you don't like that kind of finish, use the matte medium and your finished painting will have no gloss whatever. If you want some gloss, but not too much, you can mix the two mediums together. After a little experimenting, you'll come up with just the amount of gloss you desire. By doing this, it's possible to produce what's sometimes called a satin-like finish.

Varnishes

I can't think of a good reason for varnishing an acrylic painting. If a glossy medium has been used, the acrylic painting will look varnished anyway. Oil paintings, however, are rather fragile and should be varnished not only to bring out their color but to protect them as well.

In acrylic paints, the minute granules of pigment are encased forever in a tough, transparent layer of plastic. This plastic forms the binder for the paint. So why varnish? If you must, you have a choice between two acrylic varnishes—glossy and matte. (Just like the mediums, right?) Some manufacturers say you can use the mediums as final varnishes, so read the small print on the bottles. If you use these acrylic varnishes, remember that they're not like those used for oil paintings, which can be removed if they turn yellow or become dirty. Acrylic varnishes are for keeps.

What kind of varnish should you use for an oil painting, and when should you use it? First, let me tell you what you shouldn't use—copal varnish. While it gives oil paintings a handsome, glossy appearance, the kind I think oils should have, the experts say it's a "no-no." So I guess you'd better pass it by. And remember that no final varnish should go on an oil painting until it's dry—really dry—and that may take several months or even a couple of years.

For a final varnish, damar is the one most used today. It does a good job, almost as good as copal, and the experts approve of it. Someday, I'm going to say "to hell with the experts" and varnish every picture I have around with copal. Then I'll sit down and admire the slick, shiny gloss of each one. I think the well-groomed look that copal varnish creates is as necessary to a picture as it is to a beautiful woman, but alas, they say it doesn't really protect.

Besides final protective varnish, there are also varnishes you can use for touching up your oil paintings. If these so-called "retouch" varnishes bear the name of a reliable manufacturer, they're safe and can be used as soon as your painting is dry to the touch. If an oil paint begins to look dry and dull and you want to bring it back its original wet look, this is the varnish to use.

Keep Equipment Simple

Year after year, I caution amateur painters about the quantity of materials and equipment with which they inundate themselves. Watercolor painters seem to be the worst offenders of equipment "overkill." They really load themselves down! A rather heavy, middle-aged painter struggling through loose beach sand or over slippery rocks, carrying one of those huge canvas bags large enough to hold a full sheet of paper and a drawing board, another bag or knapsack into which is packed enough materials for a month's work, plus an easel, is a sad sight indeed. But it's one I see every summer.

Someone must have sold such painters on the idea that they *must* have all that junk! They seem to think that the more stuff they carry, the fewer problems they'll have. Nothing could be further from the truth! There's really nothing complicated about the tools and equipment you need to paint a picture. All you need are some tubes of paint and painting medium, something to paint on, some brushes (not many) to apply the paint with, and something to hold the panel or canvas while you're working on it.

These major items, plus a few incidentals, are all you really need! Why carry full sheets of watercolor paper and large a board when some of the best water-colors ever painted outdoors were done on quarter sheets? Why a large palette holding twenty or more colors, when any landscape can be painted with ten or less? And don't carry a stool or folding chair unless you suffer from some physical handicap. Stand up to paint!

Minimum Outdoor Painting Kits

When you set out to paint on location, the first thing you should do is check your materials. It's not funny to arrive somewhere miles from home and find you've left your brushes behind. No, it's not the least bit amusing, except to your painting companions. They find it so funny they remind you of it for months!

Oil. Now imagine I'm about to set forth to make a sketch in oil paint. This is what I assemble before I leave home, and it should be enough for anyone. My 12″ x 16″ wooden paintbox contains the following: Nine tubes of color (those listed under *Oil Palette*) plus white, a half-dozen brushes (brights) of various sizes, some paint rags torn into 6″ squares, and a tube of Res-n-Gel. My paintbox also contains a flat, screw-top can filled with turpentine or kerosene, which I use for cleaning my brushes while I work, and a small round tin—the kind tuna fish comes in—which fits into the shallow paintbox and is a useful container to rinse brushes in. I also put in my paintbox a 6-foot length of sash cord to anchor my easel if the wind's blowing. Next come my palette, palette knife, and painting knife. If it's summer, I also take a small bottle of insect repellent. My two 12″ x 16″ Masonite panels fit in the lid of the paintbox. That's my complete kit for working in oil paint outdoors.

Acrylic. For working outdoors with acrylic, I make a few changes. I use the same 12″ x 16″ paintbox with the panels in the lid. It holds my acrylic tubes of paint in the ten colors I've listed. I take the same half-dozen brushes, paint rags, and insect repellent, but not the wooden oil palette. In its place, I use a 12″ x 16″ piece of white Formica because it's easier to clean. The palette knife and painting knife are still

Figure 3. Here's my complete watercolor sketching kit, with the contents of the knapsack and canvas envelope spread out. This is the only equipment you need for watercolor painting outdoors.

there, but the turpentine can and the small round tin are out. For acrylic painting I need only water as my medium, so I take along an old army canteen full of water and the bottom half of a plastic detergent bottle, which serves as my water cup. I attach a string handle to my "water cup" and both it and the canteen are tied securely to the paintbox, or sometimes to the easel, and that's that.

Watercolor. My watercolor kit is much simpler than the kits my students carry as they follow me around the countryside. In place of the 12″ x 16″ paintbox that I use for oil and acrylic, I put everything, or almost everything, into a small knapsack. Here's what goes into it: my combination paintbox and palette, the tobacco tin holding my paint tubes, some paper towels, a plastic sponge, four or five brushes, the army canteen filled with water, the bottom half of a plastic detergent bottle to which I've attached a string handle, part of a roll of masking tape, and a couple of razor blades (in the tobacco tin).

My paper—half and quarter-sheet sizes of both 140 and 300 lb. weights—and an unpainted Masonite panel slightly larger than a half-sheet go into a flat canvas envelope that my wife skillfully put together.

My easel, the knapsack, and the canvas envelope make just three things to carry. The knapsack has a wide shoulder strap. The canvas envelope goes under my arm. I carry the easel in my right or left hand. Now don't say you need a lot more equipment than I've indicated, because you don't, and that's the truth!

Figure 4. This is Nancy, one of my students, sitting on the ground to paint a scene in Lanesville Cove, Massachusetts.

Lanesville Cove. Watercolor on paper, 15″ x 20″. This is the place on Cape Ann that I've painted and written about so often. In fact, one or another area of Lanesville has appeared in my three previous books. In recent years, I've taken many students there to paint. This watercolor was a demonstration for a class of thirty. With so many students watching every stroke, I couldn't afford to be timid. Some of the watchers even commented on how rapidly I completed the picture—forty-five minutes, according to the official time-keeper. Then what did my students do? They sat down, after making sure they were quite comfortable, and dibbled away at their pictures for two or three hours! Getting the inexperienced painter to work rapidly outdoors is almost a hopeless task.

2 Color Characteristics and Color Mixing

Is it possible to be a good painter and yet not be a fine colorist? Yes it is! Great colorists are rare. Besides, color is a very personal matter. For example, I think of Rembrandt's work in terms of brown, Turner's and Van Gogh's as yellow, Corot's as gray-green, and Bonnard's brings me visions of violet and orange. But you may have a completely different reaction to these painters—and that's what I mean when I say color is a very personal matter.

A great many contemporary painters use such a limited palette it's tempting to think they're color blind. Of course, they're not, are they? I think it's possible to use a limited number of colors and still produce a picture that isn't just a monotonous arrangement of grays and brown. After all, if the world really were just gray and brown, it would be a sad place indeed!

Painting with three colors, or even two, is fine for study purposes. And it's an advantage when you're learning about tonal values, for instance. You don't have the problems of color and color mixing to contend with at the same time.

Color Terminology

There are six terms used to describe color which the beginner should learn: hue, value, intensity, primary, secondary, and complementary. Knowing what these six terms mean will help you mix color and plan your paintings. Unless you want to become a chemist in a paint factory, it isn't necessary to know much more about the terminology of color than this.

Hue. This is the actual color. For example, red, blue, green, and yellow are hues.

Value. This is the degree of lightness or darkness of a color. The lighter the color, the higher the value, and vice versa. When you make a dark color lighter by adding white, for example, you raise its value.

Intensity. This simply means the degree of brightness or brilliance of a color. Blue is much more intense than gray, yellow is much brighter or more intense than tan.

Primary. Red, yellow, and blue are the three primary colors. They're called primary because they can't be duplicated by mixtures of any other colors.

Secondary. These are colors that result from mixing together two primary colors. Red and yellow produce the secondary color orange, yellow and blue make green, and blue and red make violet.

Complementary. Certain colors are said to be complementary to each other. If you were to draw a color wheel describing the primary colors and the way they combine to create the secondary colors, certain colors would appear opposite each other on the circle. For example, orange and blue would be opposite each other, as would violet and yellow, and red and green. These are the complementary colors. If you mixed together any two complementary colors in the correct proportions, the result would be gray.

Warm and Cool Colors

At the risk of repeating myself, I must stress again how important it is for the student to think of color in terms of temperature—warm and cool. In landscape painting, the juxtaposition of warm and cool color creates the illusion of sunlight and shadow.

The warm colors are the yellows, reds, and browns. The cool colors are the blues, blue-greens, and violets. Of course, yellow-green is a warm color if it's predominantly yellow, and violet can be either warm or cool depending on how much red is in the mixture. I think of orange as the warmest color and of Thalo blue as the coolest.

Try this experiment with your colors to help you understand color temperature. Make the following little color charts and see how the colors seem to change when they're surrounded by other colors. First, paint four or five little squares of one color on a piece of white paper, keeping the squares about 1″ apart. Around each of the squares, paint a band of a different color. For example, paint four or five squares of orange, then surround the first with a band of blue, the second with yellow, and so on. Each band should completely enclose the square of color within it. Although the original squares are all exactly the same color, they'll seem to be different colors when surrounded by the various bands. Some will appear higher in value than their neighbors, some warmer, others cooler. By doing this, you'll learn that a color can be affected by the colors around it, and you'll see how specific colors affect each other.

Using the Correct Color Names

When you speak about colors, use their correct names—be professional. Ladies, don't be influenced by the interior decorator who becomes ecstatic about puce or periwinkle blue! The cosmetic people come up with a beauty now and then, too. To me, tangerine is a fruit, not a color. The paint manufacturer, I'm sorry to say, isn't blameless either. How about geranium lake, grenadine, peacock blue, and rose tyrein? So help me, they're listed in the catalog of a well-known manufacturer of artist's materials.

Ten Colors

As I said when I described my oil, acrylic, and watercolor palettes beginning on page 11, I think ten tubes of color in the paintbox are better than twenty. With ten colors, you can paint any type of landscape or seascape, from the brightest and most colorful to the drabbest and most monotonous. I paint from nature as simply as possible, using perhaps four or five of my ten colors in any one picture.

I don't insist that my students use my list of ten colors, although most of them seem to want to do so. It's strange that many amateurs think if they have the same equipment—brushes, knives, colors—that their teacher uses, they'll be better painters themselves.

Characteristics of Colors

Here's a little information about each of the ten colors I use on my oil palette. (Turn back to page 11 for a discussion of the variations on these basic colors for my acrylic and watercolor palettes.)

1. *Titanium white.* This is the most useful white. It seems to have replaced flake white, which contains lead and is poisonous. It has good covering power.

Sunlight and Shadow. Oil on gesso panel, 10″ x 14″. Strange and interesting things can happen to the outdoor painter. For instance, when this sketch was almost finished, the foreground wasn't as dark as it is now. The whole picture was sunny. Then a cloud appeared from out of nowhere and cast a shadow over the entire foreground to create a very dramatic effect. Could I pass up a gift like that? Of course not! In ten minutes, I re-painted the whole rocky cliff. Using a palette knife, I scraped off the paint I'd used to capture the rocks in sunlight, then painted dark tones into the paint that was left on the surface of the panel. This wasn't the first time I've been able to take advantage of sudden changes of light or weather. The landscape painter must be ready and willing—and he mustn't hesitate.

Cape Spencer. Oil on gesso panel, 12″ x 16″. This is one of the few pictures I've painted on the Canadian coast. I was lucky on that trip—it's a chancy coast for the artist. The weather may be beautiful, but the painter may also be fogged in for a week. Here, we are looking straight out to the Bay of Fundy. Charlie Mitchell, the lightkeeper, and his family lived in the house when I painted it. The lighthouse itself was hidden by the hill on the left. I think I captured the open loneliness of the New Brunswick coast here by including a large sky area and placing the horizon well below the center. I used a Masonite panel, which I'd given three coats of acrylic gesso. I had toned the gesso ground with a gray oil paint wash before I left for Canada. I used copal painting medium to thin the oil paint, putting a few drops in each mound of paint and the rest in the palette cup.

2. *Cadmium yellow light.* A brilliant, opaque yellow. It's very useful for mixing greens and for painting sunlight.

3. *Yellow ochre.* A natural earth color, dull yellow or tan. One of the most useful colors on the palette.

4. *Raw sienna.* Also an earth color, darker than yellow ochre. I can't get along without it. It's great for mixing with my blues to obtain greens.

5. *Cadmium orange.* Loosely mixed with white and cerulean blue, it produces a variety of warm and cool grays. With Thalo blue, it creates rich greens.

6. *Cadmium red light.* This is my only bright red. I seldom use it, except in autumn scenes. It's good for that "singing" touch in an otherwise cool, gray color scheme.

7. *Burnt sienna.* Although most people think of this color as brown, it's really a deep orange. This color produces unusual dark greens when mixed with blue.

8. *Burnt umber.* The fastest drying color on the oil palette, this dark, rich brown is obtained by heating raw umber. If you add a little of this color to the white you use in mixtures with other colors, it will speed up the drying of the whole picture.

9. *Cerulean blue.* A very opaque color of great density. It's useful in skies and for cool, distant tones.

10. *Thalo (phthalocyanine) blue.* A powerful color that can get into everything if you're not careful. Mixed with white, it produces a beautiful clear "sky" blue. Mixed with yellow, it produces fine greens.

White Paint

In oil paints, using too much white paint is as bad as using too much black. They both tend to deaden other colors. Pictures that convey a feeling of light to the viewer are really rich in color. You can't create the illusion of light by adding white.

When you look at color reproductions of paintings in art books, look at the margin of white paper around the picture. Then you'll see how much darker than white the lightest tones of the picture actually are. A Bonnard painting of a sunny room may appear quite high in key, but against the white paper you'll quickly see how rich it is. Pictures painted with too much white in the mixture simply look whiter. They don't seem to be filled with natural light.

It's easy to make the mistake of using too much white paint in painting outdoors, especially along the shore: the sun shines on the water, white boats bob about, the sandy beach is a blaze of light, and there are people in bright summer clothing. How gay it all is! But think before you squeeze out half a tube of white paint. *Observe*, and you'll see that all the color isn't as light as you first thought. It's quite rich after all, and you can't capture it by loading your palette or canvas with white paint.

Tube Greens

As I said earlier, I prefer to mix my greens from combinations of blues and yellows. I don't like any of the tube greens. Viridian is a nice color in itself and good as a transparent glaze in oil painting, but it has no covering power, so it's not of much use when I'm doing a fast impression from nature. Hooker's green is a color I absolutely detest, so I'll only say that it's been called the favorite green of watercolorists, although I can't imagine why.

If you must have a tube of green on your oil palette, try Thalo green. It's an intense, transparent hue. Or you might try chromium oxide green, which is an interesting, off-beat kind of olive green. If you'll only remember that colors can be mixed together to obtain other colors, your summer landscapes won't have that "green right out of the tube" look. And the greens you mix will be more personal than those you buy.

Graying Colors

When the average person thinks of gray, he thinks of a mixture of black and white. Black and white do make gray. But the artist often needs colorful grays, and he can't mix those from black and white alone. You can gray-down a color—that is, lower its intensity. You can do this by adding black to it, but a better way is to add its complementary color. For instance, you can gray a red by mixing some green with it, orange by adding blue, and yellow by adding violet. These are all mixtures of complementary colors. When you're working with opaque paint—either oil or acrylic—you can also mix white paint with your colors to produce many fine grays. Whether they're warm or cool will depend on how you vary the proportions of the colors you use. For instance, if you want a warm gray, you should allow red to dominate the mixture. You can obtain a cool gray from a mixture in which blue is the dominant color.

Contrasting bright colors against dull, or solemn, colors, and contrasting warm grays against cool grays makes bright colors look even more brilliant. It's a mistake to think that by using only bright color in a picture you can produce brilliant effects. You can't.

Darks Without Blacks

A dark tone made with black paint is dull and lifeless compared to the darks obtained from mixtures of other colors. Black is the absence of light—that is, the black pigment doesn't reflect any light. In nature, shadows aren't black. They have color, and in most of them there's reflected light from a nearby object or from the sky above.

The color of a cast shadow is also affected by the color of the surface it's cast upon. A shadow cast upon green grass isn't the same color as one cast upon a dirt road or a sandy beach. For example, imagine a large, isolated rock casting a shadow on the beach. The rock is quite warm in color, almost yellow ochre. This warm color is reflected in the shadow area close to the rock, while the shadow area farthest from the rock receives cool light from the sky.

It's best not to use black paint at all for outdoor painting in any medium. If you don't have it in your paintbox, you won't be tempted to use it. For a deep, rich dark in oil or acrylic, I often use a mixture of alizarin crimson, which is a deep, transparent, rosy red, and Thalo blue. Full strength, this mixture is as dark as black, but not as "dead." It's really a very dark purple. You can also use Thalo blue and burnt umber to produce a good dark that resembles black, but I think the first combination has more life.

Burnt sienna mixed with either Thalo or ultramarine blue makes a rich, dark green tone. I use it when I paint trees, especially the dark pines and other evergreens along the coast. Raw sienna mixed with these blues also makes a nice, dark green, though not as dark as the mixture made with burnt sienna. Watercolorists often use Payne's gray to produce darks. There's nothing really wrong with this, except that it's a ready-mixed color and contains black (along with ultramarine blue, and a touch of yellow ochre). If you do use Payne's gray, keep in mind that it dries much lighter than it appears when wet. With the exception of alizarin crimson, I find that the mixtures mentioned above work as well in watercolor as they do in oil and acrylic.

Penobscot No. 3. Watercolor on Bristol paper, 11½″ x 22½″. This is one of many paintings and sketches I made in this area. I think it's sometimes necessary to break out of a rut and get away from standard sizes such as the half-sheet of watercolor paper and the 16″ x 20″ canvas. I think this subject lends itself to the long, horizontal shape I used here. I painted it on very smooth Bristol paper. An artist can't dawdle when he's working on smooth paper. The washes dry so fast on it that the painter is forced to work rapidly, and perhaps that's a good reason to try it.

Surf at Bailey. Oil on watercolor paper, 16″ x 20″. This is the first marine painting I ever did. I painted it at Bailey Island, Maine, in 1947. I was quite excited about surf painting at that time. Of course, I knew nothing about it, but I was quite willing to try. It was also my first trip to the Maine coast, and I found it to be very much like parts of my old home in Cornwall. Today, I doubt that I could paint with the reckless abandon I used in painting this subject. Except for the sky and the distant water, I did the entire painting with a painting knife, using 300 lb. watercolor paper which I sized with shellac thinned with denatured alcohol. The thick, rich impasto has held up well—there isn't one crack in the surface of the paint. The paper, by the way, was fastened to a plywood panel with masking tape. A marine painting specialist could probably criticize the action of the water, but I was young and daring when I painted it. It was fun to do then, and it's fun to see it now, after all these years.

3   *Water, Smooth and Rough*

When I was planning this book, a friend suggested that I write a chapter on painting water—smooth and rough, deep and shallow. I wish now that I hadn't fallen into such a trap, because I don't think it's possible to explain *how* to paint a particular type of water. If I did that, I'd be laying down a formula or recipe, and that's the last thing I want to do. A painting based entirely on how-to-do-it formulas is a deadly thing indeed. Painting water is like painting any other aspect of nature. The variety of water's effects is infinite and there are no set procedures for painting them. I can only point out the things you should observe and tell you that good, realistic painting is based on good observation.

In all honesty, I must admit that I think the best way to learn to paint water is to go to nature and observe the ocean in all its moods. Sketch it in paint or pencil. Learn the anatomy of waves. And do this in all seasons of the year, year after year. This is what the great marine painters did. America's two greatest marine painters, Winslow Homer and Frederick Waugh, lived beside the sea. Homer lived on the coast of Maine and Waugh lived first in St. Ives in Cornwall, England, and then in Provincetown, Massachusetts. They were specialists, and I think the kind of marine painting they did is a job for specialists!

However, if you're sure you want to spend the rest of your life painting the ocean as it pounds the shore, more power to you! If you're interested enough—and I might add, talented enough—you may become a good marine painter. And I'll be the first to applaud your courage.

The Color of Water

Let's first consider the color of water. On a bright, clear day when the ocean is bluer than blue, dip up a glassful of water and hold it up to the light. It isn't blue—in fact, it has no color. So why is a mass of it blue! The color of water depends on several factors: the depth of the water, the character of the bottom, and most of all on the color of the sky. Ripples on the surface of the water reflect this color. If the water is absolutely calm and flat, you won't see any sky color reflected in it. Rough, deep water along the coast is very blue when the sky above is blue—very blue, indeed. (How do you think the color *ultra*marine blue got its name!) On days when the sky is gray, the ocean is also gray—so don't paint a lead-gray sky and a blue ocean!

Where the ocean meets the beach, the water becomes shallow and its color is also influenced by the ocean bottom. On a sandy shore, the waves pick up sand as they roll shoreward. When the sky is blue, the waves are the warm color of the sand mixed with the blue of the sky and topped by the white of the foam. However, if the shallow water is contaminated or filled with silt that's been washed into it by a stream or river, it will probably be too opaque to be influenced by the color of the sand at the bottom. It will be the color of the churned-up mud, with some touches of blue if there's a blue sky above it.

The Coast at Zennor. Oil on gesso panel, 9″ x 12″. This is prehistoric Cornwall, the remote, boulder-strewn, heather-and-bracken-covered moors that stretch for ten miles between St. Ives and Land's End. The curious who are willing to explore will find stone circles, Cromleches, and remains of ancient villages. It was from here that D. H. Lawrence wrote enthusiastic letters to Katherine Mansfield, imploring her to join him in the land of Tristram and Iseult. I was born a few miles from here and I've sketched and painted the moors and magnificent cliff scenery many times. It's my favorite part of Cornwall. The view here is looking west toward Ireland. A composition that takes in so much terrain must be carefully designed. Students, note that I've placed my horizon well above the center and that the three main shapes—sky, ocean, and land—differ in size from one another. Collection Mr. and Mrs. Lee D. Hines.

Gurnard's Head. Oil on cardboard, 16″ x 20″. All artists, when they make painting trips abroad, and especially when plane travel is necessary, are faced with the problem of transporting their materials. Unless one is close to a large town or city, artist's supplies are difficult to find in Europe. I've learned from experience to travel light. I often do paintings such as this one on lightweight cardboard that I prepare with a ground of acrylic gesso, front and back. Two dozen of these panels fit easily into my suitcase. While I'm painting on them, I clip the cardboard to Masonite panels. Since these cardboard sketches aren't considered permanent, I repaint the best pictures on canvas when I return home. This beautiful headland, named for a fish, lies halfway between St. Ives and Land's End in Cornwall. Collection of Mr. and Mrs. Carroll W. Pratt.

When the ocean water flows over rock ledges covered with seaweed (called rockweed), it seems to take on deep green tones as you look through it to the rockweed below. When the sky is gray, the sand or seaweed below the water still has some effect on the color, but it's not as intense as it is on a clear day.

The position of the sun in the sky also has an effect on the color of water. At sunset, as the orb of the sun dips toward the horizon, the areas of the water that reflect the sun are a warm color that can be anything from gold to ruby red. To the left and right of the sun's reflection the water may be quite cool in color, with deep blues and violets appearing cold in contrast to the intense red, yellow, and orange of the sun's reflection.

Perspective in Water

The amateur painter sometimes finds it difficult to paint receding water in the correct perspective—that is, to make the water appear more and more distant as it goes off toward the horizon. This is especially difficult when you're looking seaward from the beach. Just remember that the ocean has a flat, or level, surface, and keep it all on one plane. Then create the effect of receding water by making a gradual change from fairly dark tones in the foreground to lighter tones toward the horizon, or vice versa. This will help establish the correct perspective and keep the ocean from appearing to rise up like a blue wall.

Painting Smooth Water

It's best to paint smooth water in oil or acrylic, using horizontal brush strokes. I suggest that you use short, choppy strokes in the distance and larger strokes in the foreground. It's a good idea to use a fairly large brush for this.

When I'm painting a large area of smooth water in watercolor, I first indicate the water with a flat wash, trying to match the middle tone in the water and remembering that watercolor dries lighter than it appears when it's wet. When the first wash is dry, I often use some drybrush along the horizon to represent distant ripples. The paint I use for the drybrush must be lower in value than the underwash if it's to show up. If I want to add a sparkle of light on the distant water, I wait until the washes are completely dry and scrape out the highlight with the flat edge of a razor blade.

Observing Rough Water

I think painting rough water is more difficult than painting smooth water because the action or movement of the water must also be suggested. The best way to learn to paint rough water is to watch it and observe the anatomy of the waves. But I'll tell you how to study it just enough to create acceptable paintings without first going through agonizing years of serious study. Bear in mind that I said "acceptable paintings." You can do those even if you live in Iowa—your friends and relations will like them, although museum curators won't fall over one another to acquire your work.

Here's what you do. If you don't live on the coast, spend your vacation there. Pick a place where you're likely to find surf. Southern California is a likely place on the West Coast, and there's Oregon in the North. On the East Coast, you've a choice between Cape Cod, where you'll find sandy beaches and dunes, and Cape Ann with its rocks and ledges. And, of course, there's also the rockbound coast of Maine. The best times of year to visit the beaches on the East Coast are spring and late fall. There's not much chance that you'll find rough water there in midsummer.

Beach Pool, St. Agnes. Oil on gesso panel, 9″ x 12″. This is an impression of the Cornish coast at St. Agnes Head. I omitted the cottages that mar the beauty of this splendid headland. This place, with its great sandy beach and the pools of saltwater left by the receding tide, is a summer treat for children—and for artists. I tried here to convey a feeling of the marvelous diffused light found along this coast. I used quite a lot of broken color in this sketch, although it can't be seen in this black and white reproduction. The side of the cliff is a mingling of warm and cool colors—blue, orange, and both raw and burnt sienna, weaving together like a tapestry. The colors of both sky and cliff are reflected in the pool. A suggestion of tiny distant figures sets the scale of the scene.

Ballinskelligs Bay. Watercolor on paper, 8½″ x 11½″. If you've ever ridden around the Ring of Kerry in Southern Ireland, you probably stopped at Ballinskelligs Bay for a spot of tea or a touch of something stronger. It's a beautiful place, tranquil yet with a feeling of wildness. There was a cold wind blowing the day I was there with a Painting Holiday group. In fact, one courageous lady and I were the only members of the party to brave the open beach. The others sketched from the windows of the bus we traveled in. This watercolor is the result of an uncomfortable half hour spent fighting the wind. But I've made some of my best outdoor sketches under even worse conditions. It doesn't pay to get too comfortable. I used some opaque white in the sky and foreground, but left the white paper untouched for the lights of the houses, the sandy beach, and the water. In the foreground, I used some spatter work to suggest smaller pebbles between the large rocks.

Up from the Beach. Watercolor on paper, 15″ x 20″. I painted this directly onto dry, 140 lb., rough watercolor paper. The rough grain had quite an influence on the brushwork, as you can easily see if you compare this to the watercolors in this book that I painted on smooth-surfaced paper. Like the young George Washington, I cannot tell a lie—at least not about this picture! It's the only one in this book that I didn't paint on the coast or from material gathered at the coast. But I've seen places exactly like this on the coast of Maine, wonderful areas where the forest ends and the beach begins, strewn with a jumble of uprooted trees, dried mounds of seaweed, and driftwood cast up by the ocean. Where did I paint this? A long way from the ocean, at Oak Creek Canyon, Arizona! Sorry 'bout that, but I've included it here because it's one of my favorites—and I could've fooled you!

The White Boat. Watercolor on paper, 7½″ x 10″. I sketched this small watercolor for a group of students at Boothbay Harbor, Maine. It was a demonstration on painting water and reflections. Notice that the spontaneous brushwork creates a feeling of movement in the water and that the reflection of the boat is lower in value than the boat itself. This creek leads inland a short distance from the harbor. Its banks are quite picturesque, as such places often are. When I was there, it had become a resting place for all kinds of discarded gear. There was a sunken old boat just out of the picture on the right, and still farther on were the remains of a wooden landing. There was even a heron perched on one leg waiting for an unsuspecting fish to come by. It was a quiet backwater area, loaded with subjects for the artist to paint.

If you don't know how to take a good color photograph of things in motion, you should learn before you leave home, because that's the key to this operation. What I'm suggesting isn't difficult. Every year, people take thousands of color slides on vacation and bore their friends back home with them. Just point your camera at the oncoming wave and click the shutter. The result should be like the one on p. 150. It's a transparency that I shot at Andrews Point on Cape Ann. I'm no genius with a camera—far from it—but as you can see, the picture turned out well.

If you make slides or transparencies as I do, you can look at them in a viewer or, better yet, project them onto a screen or a sheet of white paper. The wave's motion will be "suspended" for you. The wave won't move, and there'll be no confusion created by one wave following another, or by the wave's dissolving into foam. It'll be right there posing for you, as many times as you wish to look at it. Use the photograph as reference, but then try to inject something personal into your painting. The photo is there only to help you see the action and anatomy of the wave, to help you avoid the frustration and confusion you'd surely experience if you tried to paint a rough sea directly from nature. I'll have more to say about the use of photography in Chapter Twelve.

Surface Patterns and Textures

As a rule, patterns on the surface of the water are created by the wind. A slight breeze close to the surface is enough to change the character of a large or even a small area. The little ripples "kicked up" by the breeze may contain as many as a million or two vertical walls. When the vertical sides of the ripples are back-lighted—that is, viewed *against* the light source—they may form a pattern on the surface of the water that's darker in tone than the surrounding flat surface, which reflects the light. When these vertical walls are front-lighted, they'll reflect the light and may very well form a lighter pattern against the surrounding water. These patterns and textures are a great help in painting. They can be used to establish the plane of the water by contrasting against it—so watch for them and use them.

Reflections in the Water

Reflections seldom appear in straight marine painting. (I mean the "rock-and-surf" pictures I'll discuss later on in this chapter.) The water in those pictures is usually too rough to reflect the sky, the sun, or boats. However, you'll have to deal with reflections often as you paint harbors where the water is calm and reflects the boats and dockside buildings. Painting reflections shouldn't be a great problem if you observe them carefully and remember that the color of the reflection is usually very close to the color of the object itself.

Why do so many amateur painters make all reflections blue, no matter what color the reflected object really is? "But I thought reflections were supposed to be blue," one of my lady students once remarked. She had gone merrily through life without giving serious thought to, or making any careful observations of, what she was painting. She was quite surprised when I pointed out to her that the reflection of a dirty, gray lobster boat was a slightly darker gray, and that of a lobsterman in yellow oilskins was a modified version of that yellow. It was a typical case of someone who had never learned to see trying to express herself in a visual art! As you paint, observe the color of the object. Its reflection will probably be that color, mixed with the color of the sky.

There are books available that contain scientific explanations of reflections, complete with diagrams to illustrate how they look and why they are as they are.

Seaside Goldenrod. Watercolor on paper 9½″ x 12½″. The wild goldenrod is plentiful on the East Coast in autumn. Its yellow blossoms brighten the roadsides and fields everywhere. It's my favorite flower, and I've often included it in my coastal sketches. I like the way its warm yellow flower complements the gray of the rocks and the blue of the ocean. My procedure for painting this picture was to first paint everything but the goldenrod. When the grassy background dried, I painted the blossoms with acrylic white straight from the tube. I allowed this to dry, then painted over it a wash of cadmium yellow watercolor paint. Most of the picture is a very dry rendering, done with plenty of paint and very little water on the brush. In the foreground, you can see some fingernail scratches.

Marina. Watercolor on paper, 10″ x 14″. This picture illustrates how the camera can be used to capture effects that would be impossible to paint from nature. This shows a small part of Stamford Marina shortly before sunset. We'd spent the day cruising Long Island Sound with Rose and Bill Strosahl. It was a lovely day, with high-flying clouds and the bluefish biting. While I was helping Bill make fast at the anchorage, I turned and saw this gorgeous sight. The sun was rapidly sinking behind the boats, creating different lighting effects almost every minute. I ran for the camera and pointed it over the stern just in time. By the time I returned the camera to the cabin, it was dark. Artists often paint these fleeting effects from memory. I have myself. However, the camera can be a useful tool if used with discretion—as a tool and not a crutch.

Lifting Fog. Oil on canvas, 16″ x 20″. This is another of those "rock and surf" pictures I was fond of painting thirty years ago but can't seem to work up much feeling for today. Such paintings are considered to be a job for the specialist, and the painters who do them make the subject their life's work. In the days when I painted this, I used to go wherever any of Frederick Waugh's marine paintings were on view, and I even went just to see the work of his imitators. Waugh was so popular that he had as many imitators then as Wyeth has today. After awhile, however, I lost interest. It got so monotonous—after all, how many different ways are there to paint a wave and some rocks? Anyway, this is a fair example of what I was doing then. I painted it at Cape Elizabeth, Maine, on a foggy day. This one is exclusively brushwork, no painting knifework. Notice how the brushstrokes follow the forms of both the water and the rocks.

Not being of a mathematical turn of mind, I must confess they baffle me. I disregard the scientific theories, and having a well-trained eye when it comes to landscape and seascape, I depend on good observation and put down on paper or canvas what I see in nature. If you want a more exact explanation of reflections, I suggest you go to the library. But if you want to paint them in a manner that will show others how interesting you find them, how beautiful they are, and how you as an artist *feel* about them, go to nature, as all serious outdoor painters have done.

Composing Tidal Pool Pictures

When you're painting the coast don't neglect the tidal pools as possible subject matter. As water pours over on rocky ledges, it wears away indentations—bowls, if you like—in the rocks and these hold the seawater left there by the outgoing tide. Some of these tidal pools are small, others are quite large, and they're all interesting.

Sometimes, several rocks form a wall or barrier to create a pool about two feet deep. This is the best kind of tidal pool to paint. Small shellfish cling to its steep sides and lie along its bottom. Here, barnacles, open, and waving tentacles, small snail-like periwinkles, and blue-black mussel shells contrast beautifully against the warm tones of the rocks. There are also various types of seaweed, free-floating or growing from clefts in the rock walls. Small fish dart about in some of these pools, adding movement to all the beauty.

And beauty it is—but a kind of beauty that's the very devil to paint. Many have tried but few have succeeded in putting it on canvas. How should you go about painting this bewitching subject? First, consider the composition. If you paint only the pool without including any of the rock's surface (I mean the rock you're *standing* on, of course), you may have a good painting, depending on your ability as an artist. But the picture might lack depth. I think it's best to show some of the rock's top surface, as well as at least one side of the rock descending into the water. The rest of the design will depend on the contents of the pool and how you use them.

Painting Tidal Pools

One painting method watercolorists and acrylic painters might try is to first paint the contents of the tidal pool—seaweed, shellfish, and sand—and forget about painting the water for the moment. When this underpainting is dry, paint some transparent washes, preferably greens and blues, over it to create the illusion of water. Use acrylic paints and watercolor techniques for this kind of painting. If you use watercolor paints, you'll disturb the underpainting as you apply the wet overpainting. You can also use this approach with oil paints, but the process will take much longer because the oil underpainting will have to be quite dry before you can apply transparent oil glazes over it.

Of course, you can paint the subject using alla prima, or direct painting, but the success of such a picture depends on an exact matching of the tonal values and very careful observation of color. Even then it takes some skill and courage to pull it off, because alla prima painting must be done very quickly and with very little altering of the initial colors or brushwork. Anyway, you'll find tidal pools lovely to look at even if you never try to paint one.

"Rock-and-Surf" Pictures

Before I conclude this chapter, I feel I must add a few words about "rock-and-surf" pictures, whose subject matter most of us think of as the typical marine paint-

Fog. Oil on gesso panel, 8″ x 12½″. If you're an artist, a real painter, you won't stay indoors because the sun isn't shining. The landscape artist should study weather—all kinds of weather. Of course, sunshine and shadow are lovely to paint, but so are the subtle tones of a rainy or foggy day. I painted this small sketch in fifteen minutes on a Rockport beach, and I think it was worth doing. No, it won't set the world on fire or stand out in an exhibition, but I like to think it may have some qualities that Whistler would have admired. I first painted the three main values—sky, water, and sand—matching the colors and tones of nature as closely as possible. Then I added the light tone of the foam where the ocean meets the beach and finally the few dark notes, being careful not to make them too dark or to use too many.

A Salt Marsh. Oil on gesso panel, 14″ x 20″. From time to time, I like to experiment with various techniques. This picture is one of my attempts to paint in what I fondly imagine is the technique used by some members of the American Hudson River School. The smooth surface of a gesso-primed Masonite panel lends itself quite well to this approach. Of course, those old timers didn't have Masonite, and they must have used very finely textured canvas. I used soft brushes throughout the painting, because rugged brushwork wouldn't have created the effect I wanted. The painters of the Hudson River School didn't believe in revealing the "handwriting" of the artist—that is, using such distinctive brushwork that the artist could be recognized by that alone. The scene was the important thing to them, not how it was painted. Nowadays, the reverse seems to be true.

ing. I must confess I'm not overly fond of such pictures, even when they're well done. I say this because, if I had one hanging on my living room wall, I think it would be too much of an eyetrap. Just waiting for that oncoming wave to roll over and hit the rock would drive me mad. Perhaps that's why, although I've painted several "typical" marine paintings, I haven't exhibited any of them.

I've suggested that student marine artists use a camera in their work. However, keep in mind that this isn't a method used by professionals. No marine painting done from a photograph can ever have the authority of a painting done by a specialist who's lived by the sea and observed it day after day for years.

In my opinion, the greatest marine painter since Winslow Homer was the late Jay Connaway. He believed in soaking up knowledge of the sea outdoors, then painting the picture in the studio. His pictures have feeling, or mood, if you like. There's never the effect of a stop-action, frozen wave in Connaway's paintings.

Song of the Sea. Watercolor on paper, 15″ x 20″. This spectacular rock formation, seen here at low tide, is located near Land's End in Cornwall. The reason for its musical name is that the tides rush through this great natural archway, which leads into a pool-filled grotto, and produce sounds that suggest music. When I was a boy roaming this coast, the pool was surrounded with sand ground from pure white shells. When I visited the place a few years ago, it was covered with gummy black oil—no doubt spilled by a tanker off shore. Perhaps the ocean has cleaned up the mess by now. I certainly hope so, because it's a very lovely place. In this painting, which I did from a photograph, I tried to depict the area as it was long ago. I painted this on very smooth paper—Bristol board, which has a shiny, slick surface. I used a razor blade to scrape into the wet paint. This is a good method to use to create unusual textures.

Cliffs at Land's End. Watercolor on paper, 11″ x 15″. There are spectacular rocks and cliffs to be sketched and painted along this part of the Cornwall coast. Just off shore at the base of the cliffs stand rocks that bear names suggested by their shapes, such as the Spire, the Kettle Bottom, the Shark's Fin, the Irish Lady, the Armed Knight, and Dr. Syntax's Head. Two miles at sea is the Longships Lighthouse, standing fifty feet high atop a sixty-foot rock. Turner found the area fascinating, and so have hundreds of other artists. I introduced Rockport painter Tom Nicholas to Land's End when we visited Cornwall together several years ago. I painted this watercolor from an old sketch. I used the new Strathmore Aquarius non-buckling watercolor paper. The picture has deep rich color, and it also has a strong pattern of tonal values that I feel shows up well in black and white.

4 Shores: Some Rockbound, Some Not

Most of the shorelines I've painted are along the coast of New England, where I've spent most of my life, and along the coast of Cornwall, England, where I was born and where I made my first painting attempts. I've returned to Cornwall several times on painting trips, and I've been thrilled every time by the tremendous cliffs and charming hidden coves there.

Those great cliffs and rocky forelands that W. H. Hudson called "castles by the sea" make dramatic subject matter. I hope I've conveyed the mood to you in my pictures throughout this book. In *Gurnard's Head*, reproduced on page 35, I think I captured Cornwall's summer mood, for example. The subject of this painting is about half-way between St. Ives and Land's End, a ten-mile coastal area that could keep a painter busy for a lifetime!

British artists have painted, settled, and formed art colonies in this area since the early 1800's. They've been attracted not only by the shoreline landscape but also by the quality of light there. Among the painters who've worked there are such famous names as Whistler, Anders Zorn, Richard Sickert, and Frederick Waugh.

It was in the harbor at St. Ives that I saw naturalist painter Charles Simpson painting gulls when I was twelve years old. And it was on that day that I decided to be a painter. Since then, I've painted a lot of shoreline and coastal scenery on both sides of the Atlantic. And, of course, I've painted other subjects, too. I think the landscape painter should be interested in all aspects of nature, not just in one isolated part. Again, that's an area for the specialist.

Figure 5. This drybrush sketch shows an area of the coast in the Bay of Fundy.

Shoreline Composition

When you're painting rocks, dunes, and ocean along the shore, consider the composition carefully. Don't place the rocks and the ocean too close together. Beginners' paintings of sand dunes fail more often because the composition is poor than for any other reason.

When you're planning your picture, avoid placing two dunes or rocks of equal size on opposite sides of the canvas. If you must have two dunes or two rocks with a glimpse of the sea between them make one much smaller than the other. Better yet, use only one—or better still—paint from a vantage point on top of a tall dune or rock or from a low spot on the beach. Look for ways to avoid the commonplace, the obvious.

And for heaven's sake, don't try to include too much terrain! Resist the temptation to paint a "grand view," especially if you're using watercolor. John Singer Sargent, a master of watercolor, had a great eye for selecting subject matter for his paintings. Many of his best are what we'd call "close-ups" today. If you look at some of the paintings reproduced in *Sargent Watercolors*, by Donelson F. Hoopes, you'll appreciate Sargent's remark to a friend who urged him to paint a "view." He said, "I can't paint views. I can paint objects; I can't paint views." It's very easy to fall into the trap of taking in too much when you're face to face with nature. We all do it—I know I have. But in the end, it's the intimate subject that pleases me most.

Designing Foregrounds

When you go outdoors and look at the landscape, where do you look? At the center of the view in front of you, of course! You don't really take in every detail in the foreground, and that's why an overdeveloped foreground always looks false. The foregrounds in John Constable's outdoor sketches and in those of other 19th-century English landscape painters are fine, simple statements. When these gentlemen worked their sketches up into large pictures for the Royal Academy annual exhibition, they felt they had to "furnish" the foregrounds with vines, plants, and even wild flowers, and they often painted these with meticulous detail. What a mistake! The results were landscapes with still life foregrounds that destroyed the oneness of the pictures.

Remember, you can't look down and up at the same time. So don't overdo your foregrounds. If you're painting pebbles, for example, don't paint too many of them. If you do, it'll be difficult for the viewer to "enter" your picture. Design your foregrounds in a manner that leads the viewer's eye to the middle of the scene, which is the best place to put your point of interest. (I'll discuss the point of interest in more detail in Chapter Eleven.) Try to do this even if you have to take some liberties with nature.

Mixing Warm Colors for Rocks

No matter where you find them, rocks are rocks and cliffs are cliffs. Some are large, others small, but most of their characteristics remain the same. The only aspect in which they differ is color.

The rocks around Cape Ann and Gloucester, Massachusetts, are quite warm in color. When I paint there, I use mixtures that produce warm grays and tans. In oil paints, I've found a mixture of cadmium orange and cerulean blue with a touch of white is quite useful. This must be a very loose mixture, because if the colors are mixed too thoroughly the result may be a muddy green. But loose mixture produces a broken color. The threads of orange, blue, and white intermingle to create a color vibration that can't be obtained by smashing colors together with a palette knife or scrubbing the life out of them with a brush. Yellow ochre, burnt sienna, and burnt umber are also useful in mixing warm colors for rocks. The last two in particular produce good results when mixed with cerulean blue and white.

With the exception of cadmium orange, you can use the colors I've already listed to paint rocks in both watercolor and acrylic. However, the mixture of broken color I use in oil painting can't be made as easily with watercolor or acrylic paints. The heavy body of the oil paint itself and the impasto treatment I use lend themselves to broken color. Whereas oil is the mixing medium in oil paints, water is the mixing medium of watercolor and acrylic. Water causes the pigments to mix together thoroughly, and the effect of broken color is lost. Of course, you could try thickening acrylic paints with gel to make them behave more like oil paints. But I think if you want the picture to look like an oil painting, you should use oil paint.

Mixing Cool Colors for Rocks

Farther north in Maine, the rocks are different in color from the warm tones found on Cape Ann. They're a cold gray, almost black in some areas, and they actually look more "northern." Mars black mixed with burnt or raw umber, cerulean blue, and white is quite useful in suggesting the cold gray of these rocks. Broken color isn't necessary, as the rocks themselves have an overall gray appearance.

Painting the Form of Rocks

When you're painting rocks, don't depend too much on the use of color to describe them. Rocks have weight and bulk—they're solid. Color, no matter how interesting, won't help if your rock lacks form, or a feeling of solidity. How can you create this illusion? Simply observe the value relationships on the rock. The top of the rock is exposed to the sky and receives the greatest amount of light; the vertical sides receive less light. The part of the rock that faces away from the light source is the darkest area. When correctly stated, these value relationships impart a feeling of solidity and reality to the rock, no matter what your choice of color. Figure 6 is a drybrush drawing of rocks. Although I used only one color in the entire painting, the rocks have form because I observed the value relationships.

Of course, value study isn't quite as simple as this. You can't paint every rock on the shore as a top-lighted cube! They have a variety of sizes and shapes, some are in sunlight, and some are in shadow. There's reflected light as well as direct light. When you get out there on the shore as a beginning student, you'll find it's pretty bewildering. Believe me, I know how confusing it can be! Just keep the things your teachers have told you in the back of your mind, then relax and paint. Don't analyze the fun of painting. Working from nature should be a pleasurable experience, not a time of suffering!

Making Rocks Look Wet

When my students ask me how to paint rocks so that they look wet, I tell them to think about *why* the rocks appear wet. First of all, only the tops of the rocks look wet, because the water stays there in the shallow indentations in the rock, while it runs right off the sides. It's this thin layer of water that reflects the light from the sky to make the rocks look wet. And it's also the reason that the top of a rock may appear quite cool while its sides appear much warmer. So, to make rocks look wet, just paint the reflections of the sky—whether it's blue or gray—into the rock surfaces that face upward.

Figure 6. This is a drybrush drawing of the rock ledges at Andrews Point, Pigeon Cove, Massachusetts. The rocks have form because I observed the value relationships as I sketched them.

Tiny droplets of water on the seaweed and barnacles also cling to the side of the rock and sometimes reflect the sky or the sun. It's best to render these as small dots of both warm and cool color, placed in an irregular pattern. If you're using oil paint, you can create this effect by loading a palette knife with a fairly light tone and dragging the flat side of the knife quickly over a darker underpainting.

I must warn you that no matter how many technical tricks you learn and use, they won't help you a bit unless you also learn to observe tonal values. More than any other element, it is the correct relationship of the values that makes a painting realistic. So give it some serious thought and constantly compare the values in one part of a painting to those in another as you proceed.

Texturing Rocks

The palette knife can be a very useful tool to create texture when you're painting rocks in oil. Dragging the flat edge of a razor blade over damp watercolor also creates a convincing rock texture (Figure 7). However, beware of overdoing tricks of this kind. A little of such treatment goes a long way.

It's easy to create texture in acrylic because the paint dries so rapidly. Hold a square, flat brush almost parallel to the painting surface and drag it over dry or half-dry paint to produce a scumble or drybrush effect. You can also use this technique with oil, to paint a dark texture over a light tone or vice versa (Figure 8).

Painting Pebbles

Now let's leave the subject of large rocks for awhile and consider the pebbles found close to the water's edge. Pebbles are small or fairly small rocks that have been constantly buffeted by the ocean until they resemble stone eggs or even tennis balls. I have two pebbles the size of footballs in my garden that are so perfect in shape it's hard to believe the hand of man had nothing to do with shaping them. The cove where I found them contained hundreds more of all sizes, some of them too heavy to lift. In Figure 9, I've painted them so that you too can appreciate what a great sculptor the mighty ocean can be.

When you're painting a beach full of pebbles, don't try to paint the individual stones. It would be an impossible task. Suggest them with the use of lines, drybrush, and spatter if you're working in watercolor (Figure 10). In oil, you can use thick impasto with staccato strokes in a variety of shapes and sizes. Even though pebbles are small—some are no larger than a pea—they do have areas of light and shadow, with warm color in the lights and cool color in the shadows. These areas are most obvious when they're more or less side-lighted, as they are in the early morning or evening when the sun is low on the horizon. When the sun is high overhead at noon, contrasts of light and shadow aren't as apparent. I think beach pictures are most interesting when they're painted before ten in the morning or after three in the afternoon.

Painting Sandy Beaches and Dunes

Where do you find a shore that's sandy rather than rockbound or pebbled? Although New England is a rocky area, it has plenty of sandy beaches to paint—and sand dunes, too. When I lived in New York City, I did my shore painting on Long Island, which is actually a huge sand bar that protects the Connecticut shore.

You should paint your pictures of sandy shores in a high key to give them a feeling of reality. Make the shadows on the beach light and luminous, because they receive a great deal of reflected light. Avoid the mistake of making the sand too

Figure 7. You can use a razor blade to scrape textures into wet watercolor paint. The rougher the paper, the more varied and interesting the texture will be.

Figure 8. You can create a scumble effect in acrylic or watercolor paint by loading a square, flat brush with paint and dragging it over a dry or half-dry underpainting. You can either apply the light paint over the dark (left) or the dark paint over the light (right).

Figure 9. These egg-shaped pebbles have been sculptured by nature—ground and polished by the ocean—and are now in my garden.

Figure 10. When you're painting a pebbled beach in watercolor, you can suggest the pebbles with squiggly brushstrokes and some spatter work.

October, Hendrick's Head. Oil on cardboard, 9″ x 12″. I like the beach at the end of summer. The trees along the coast are no longer summer green, and on sunny days the ocean is bluer than blue. The beach also has more to interest the painter at this time of year. On the beach in this scene, there was a long line of seaweed left high and dry by the outgoing tide. I think its shape, widest in the foreground and becoming narrower as the mass recedes, imparts a feeling of depth to the picture. The little figures, although simply stated with a few brushstrokes, help establish the scale. After sketching the composition, I began painting the sky and worked downward, finishing each area as I went along. The last thing I did was to use some spatter work on the beach. The landscape painter learns his trade by doing sketch after sketch of this kind. Some end up in frames and are sold, others end up in the fireplace.

yellow. Sand is seldom, if ever, yellow. On the beach and in the dunes it's really a variety of warm and cool grays. When I'm painting with oil, I use a loose mixture of cadmium orange, cerulean blue, and white to create broken color. You can also try raw and burnt umber—but hold back on those yellows! If you need yellow, use yellow ochre, not one of the cadmiums.

Determining Values on the Beach

Amateur painters have trouble painting beach subjects because they find it difficult to judge value relationships in the strong sun light on the beach. As a rule, they paint the sky too dark and the sand too light.

Here's a simple device that can take the guesswork out of determining values. Start with a piece of cardboard a little larger than a standard postcard. Make a hole the size of a dime in the center of the cardboard. Make another hole halfway between the first hole and the upper edge of the cardboard. Then make a third hole halfway between the first hole and the lower edge, so that you have three holes in a vertical line (Figure 11).

Hold up the cardboard so that you can see the sky through the top hole, the sea through the center hole, and the sand through the lowest one. By looking at these three spots of color apart from their surroundings, you'll be able to determine easily where the lightest light and darkest dark are. And you'll often find that the sandy beach you thought was the lightest light is actually darker than the sky.

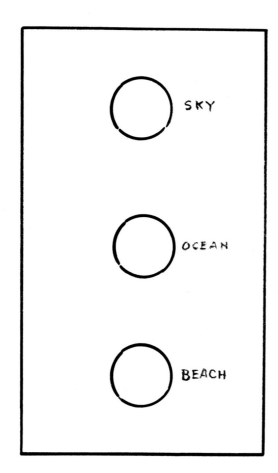

Figure 11. This simple device will help you determine value relationships on the beach. Take a piece of cardboard a little larger than a postcard and make one hole in the center. Then make two more holes, one centered above and one below the first hole. You'll be able to see the value of the sky through the top hole, the ocean through the center hole, and the beach through the bottom hole.

In Gloucester Harbor. Oil on gesso panel, 10½″ x 15″. Generations of American artists have painted in Gloucester. Winslow Homer painted some of his early watercolors there. In the days of sailboats, the harbor must have been a wonderful sight. Those Gloucester schooners, on which men fished for cod along the Grand Banks, were beautiful ships. They can be seen in the paintings of Fitz Hugh Lane, who was a native of Gloucester and is said to have been the first artist to paint its harbor. Since Lane's day, Robert Henri, George Bellows, John Sloan, and Leon Kroll have worked there. In recent years, Emil Gruppe settled at nearby Rocky Neck and has become what might be called Gloucester's official artist. I painted this sketch in front of the gallery of the North Shore Art Association, looking toward East Gloucester. I was trying to show an outdoor class how to use what I call the artist's shorthand to suggest that distant jumble of docks and shipyards.

5 *Harbors, Large and Small*

Harbors have been one of my favorite painting subjects for a long time, and understandably so. In and around a harbor, the painter finds a greater variety of colors and shapes than he can find almost anywhere else. Then, too, there's so much activity. Men in picturesque garb carry around all kinds of interesting things. They climb up and down ladders, lower buckets overside, or just stand around exchanging gossip with one another. Boats come and go often, pulling out when the artist is but half finished with his sketch, leaving the exasperated painter on the dock, mouth open and brush poised in mid-air. So beware when you set out to paint fishing boats. When their time comes to leave, they leave! I'll have more to say on boats in Chapter Six.

I think the two most often painted harbors are Lane's Cove on Cape Ann and St. Ives in Cornwall. I've painted both, but that's no claim to fame—so have countless others. I've never seen a painting of Lane's Cove by Winslow Homer, but I think he must have been there. In summers, he often painted nearby in Gloucester. The harbor of that great commercial fishing port must have been a sight to see in Homer's day! The famous Gloucester schooners that fished the Grand Banks of Newfoundland were active then. He painted them, as well as the men who went over the sides in small dories to set out the long lines for cod in all kinds of weather, running the risk of being separated from the mother ship by the fog.

The fishermen also feared being run down by one of the huge liners that crossed the Atlantic in great numbers at that time. Remember Kipling's *Captains Courageous*? The British author gathered material for this book in Gloucester. Yankee painter and English author alike found great material to work with in Gloucester.

Harbors at Low Tide

In my opinion, harbors are always more interesting to paint at low tide than they are when the tide's in. In harbors where the water level drops considerably at low tide, you can see a difference in color between the parts of the piers or wharves that are always above the high-water mark and those that are below it as high tide. Then, too, the boats are up on the mud, and the harbor's bottom is exposed in all its colorful beauty—covered with patches of sand, rock, and brown and green seaweed. There are puddles of water reflecting the sky, anchor ropes and chains, and if you're lucky, you'll see part of an old sunken boat that was submerged at high tide.

So, get yourself a tide table when you work around harbors. You can then plan to arrive on location when the tide's out—and I think you'll be glad you did!

Stone Piers

The massive granite piers and jetties of Cape Ann's harbors look very European. They remind me of Cornwall and Brittany. They provide the painter with a subject found nowhere else in the United States. Perhaps it's because stone piers

Figure 12. This is it—the one and only Motif 1, in Rockport, Massachusetts. It's one of the most popular painting subjects on the East Coast.

Figure 13. This wooden wharf, with its stiltlike pilings, is a typical sight along the coast of Maine.

are so unusual that beginners find it difficult to paint them. They have a tendency to paint the individual stones instead of first painting the entire mass of the pier in the correct value and then *suggesting* the detail. Of course, the great stone walls of Rockport, Pigeon Cove, and Lanseville are made of granite blocks placed one upon the other. However, you won't capture the essence, the feeling, by painting tidy squares with neat little cracks between them. That's the way a primitive would do it. The very fact that you're reading these words proves you're not primitive!

Wooden Wharves and Pilings

The tide has quite a drop along the coast of Maine. You won't find stone wharves there, but platforms or docks set on wooden pilings. These are quite interesting at low tide. The fishhouses and the clutter of gear seem to be held aloft on a series of stilts (Figure 13). One, not a dock but a footbridge across part of Boothbay Harbor, Maine, is a fascinating tangle of pilings at low tide. Figures crossing it at sundown with the light behind them suggest circus stilt walkers to the imaginative painter.

When you paint distant pilings, you can indicate them with just a single downward stroke. However, when you paint closer ones, you should give them some textural interest. The weathered upper parts of pilings are knotted and cracked, while the lower parts display seaweed, small shellfish, and barnacles at low tide. In Figure 13, notice how I've suggested this change between the upper and lower parts. Remember, I said *suggested*. That's the word to keep in mind when you're tempted to doodle around with detail. Don't compete with the camera! Try to paint those pilings as simply and directly as possible, using suggestive detail and textural interest at the same time. Sounds like a tall order, doesn't it? Well, I never said painting was easy!

Men at Work

There's more than boats to interest the artist around harbors. For instance, there are men at work unloading catches, painting boats, and even doing nothing. They belong in harbor pictures just as people belong in street scenes. And it's up to you to learn how to put them into your picture. You should paint them simply and directly, without detail. Try to capture the gesture or action correctly, as well as the proportions of the figures. You can paint the head with a single brushstroke, but be sure it's the correct size in relation to the rest of the figure.

Watch out for the scale relationship, too. Don't make the figure too large or too small for its surroundings. Constantly compare one part of your picture to another as you work. For instance, if there's a doorway in the picture, be sure the figure you're painting could walk through it. If there's a window, the figure should be able to look into it without standing on a box.

Harbor Gulls

A harbor without gulls is like a street without people. Gulls are the scavengers of the shore. Only city children would throw a stone at a gull—fishing folk never molest them. Watch a fishing boat as it approaches a harbor and you'll know if the catch has been good by the number of gulls following the boat. They're beggars, they're clowns, but—above all—they're beautiful. Try to spend some time sketching them as they pose, motionless, on masts and harbor pilings. And catch them in flight, too. When you put several gulls in a picture remember that they overlap one another when they're in flight. Don't make a separate little project of each one.

Big City Docks

Like city street scenes, bit city docks are best painted in the studio from pencil sketches and photographs. The press of traffic and the business of loading and unloading cargo are so hectic that the painter has little chance of setting up an easel amid the bustle. Follow the suggestions I've given you so far about working from photographs, and be sure to read *The Camera: Its Uses and Misuses*, page 127, before you start.

Cady's Chair. (Left) Acrylic on gesso-coated cardboard, 16″ x 20″. Star Island is the name of a small group of rocks on the Atlantic Avenue side of Rockport Harbor. It was the property of the late Harrison Cady, whose summer home stood just across the road. There are some old fish houses on the rocks, and on the porch of one, I found this great collection of things waiting to be painted. My daughter Elma also painted it. She later sent her picture to a New York exhibition, where it won an award. That's the reason I've never exhibited mine. I painted this picture on a piece of cardboard that had been the backing for a pad of papers. I gave it two coats of acrylic gesso on the front and one on the back. When the gesso dried, I toned the white surface with a mixture of acrylic white and raw umber thinned with water.

Sketch at Peggy's Cove. (Above) Watercolor on Bristol paper, 9″ x 12″. Now and then, though not often, I do a vignette sketch and allow the edges of the picture to wander out into an expanse of white paper. Smooth, glossy paper such as this doesn't have enough grain to contribute to the effects. However, this paper has certain advantages over the usual rough-grained watercolor paper. It's easy to remove colors from it, darks can be wiped out with a wet rag, and many interesting effects can be obtained by using a knife or razor blade on the wet paint. This type of paper isn't for everyone, but it's being used with good results by many artists. I usually prefer Strathmore regular-surfaced illustration board, which is also smooth but doesn't have the shine and polish of this "high-surface" paper.

Winter, Rockport. Opaque watercolor on paper, 9″ x 12″. Whenever I paint outdoors in winter—and I don't very often—I can't help thinking what a hardy race the American school of snow painters must have been. How well I remember the day I made this sketch from T Wharf. It was one of the fastest I ever did! It was so cold that all I could think was "What a fool I am!" and, "How fast can I get out of here?" I certainly didn't fool around with washes that needed drying time! I used opaque white paint throughout, and because I did, I finished the painting in ten minutes.

6 *Pleasure Boats and Work Boats*

You'll find boats of all shapes and sizes in and around harbors. They can usually be divided into two classes—pleasure boats and work, or lobster and fishing, boats. Among the pleasure boats, motor boats and cabin cruisers aren't very interesting subjects, although I did have good luck with my picture *Marina*, reproduced on page 43. I've the time of day to thank for that. Without that summer evening glow, the picture would have been nothing special. Sailboats have much greater appeal for the artist. They're simply more beautiful in every way than even the most expensive, deluxe motor monstrosity.

Best of all harbor subjects are the work boats—fishing craft large and small, and the lobster boats seen everywhere on the New England coast. These boats have character. They aren't all spit and polish, but they wear their working clothes with purpose and great dignity. The large, commercial fishing boats in Gloucester, called "draggers," are interesting to paint and colorful, too, with their white-topped red masts and green hulls. And these bright colors are no accident. They make the boats visible to other boats on the fishing grounds and decrease the danger of collision.

Every artist who's painted on the New England coast has also made good use of lobster boats, and for good reason. They're part of the scene. They're picturesque, and so are the lobstermen who man them. Most common among these boats are the big diesel-powered craft, the aristocrats of lobster boats. These represent large financial outlays on the parts of their owners, who are usually individuals or several members of the same family. They're powerful boats, built to stand rough winter weather a good distance from shore, and are outfitted with pulleys and winches to haul the lobster traps out of the sea.

Closer to shore, you can see lobstermen in smaller dories, hauling traps out of the water by hand. I still find it exciting to watch one of these rugged individuals riding a heavy swell in his fragile-looking boat, which is powered only by an outboard motor. With an experienced twist of the boathook, he grabs the float, pulls the ropes abroad, and hauls the trap hand over hand. The trap comes up and he removes the lobster (if indeed there is one), baits the trap, and drops it overboard again. He does all this in a few minutes, while the boat bobs up and down with the swells just a few yards away from a dangerous-looking rock ledge. It looks easy, but it's hard work.

A New Approach to an Old Subject

A Gloucester dragger out of the water for repairs is a handsome sight. The beautiful curve of its bow betrays a definite Portuguese influence. Several draggers tied up at a wharf, with nets hauled to the masthead to dry, make great picture material—so good, in fact, that I fear the subject's been overdone. Those dark green boats with their white-topped red masts and their reflections in the harbor water have become a cliché. Only the amateur and the pot-boiling artist paint them today.

Figure 14. Close to shore, lobstermen in dories haul traps out of the water by hand.

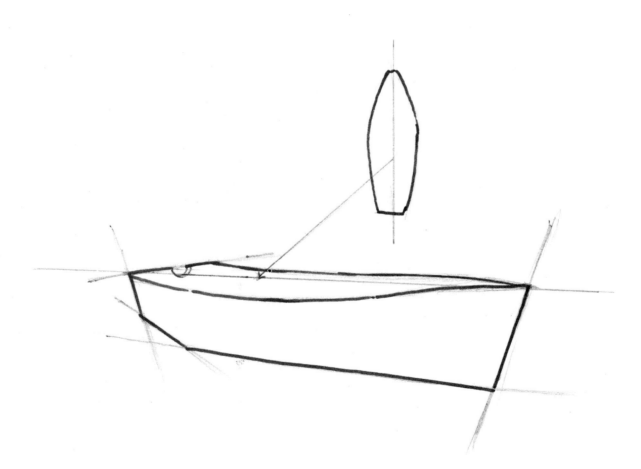

Figure 15. It's important to draw the shape and construction of boats accurately. Begin by sketching the basic form, and remember to indicate the center line, as I've done here.

But wait a minute! You don't have to do the same old composition that's been done a million times before. Use your head. Think a bit, as I did when I painted *Dragger Close-Up*, reproduced on page 91. I don't remember any painting just like it done in Gloucester harbor. I simply used a new approach to an old subject. And you can do the same with covered bridges, barns, or any other overdone subject that's become what's called "corny."

How does a subject come by that label? I suppose it originally appeals to a wide audience, then a commercial or "hack" artist begins to grind out picture after picture, making them all look pretty much alike. Then serious painters and museum curators turn against the subject because it's been overworked. Actually, however, it was always a good subject and it still is.

Drawing Boats

Sooner or later, the student or amateur artist working along the coast has to face the business of drawing a boat. There's no escaping it unless you "chicken out" and decide you're a rock and wave specialist.

You'll find that drawing boats is no more difficult than drawing anything else if you go about it in a professional way. I've already said that you can make the task of drawing a figure easier if you first understand the basic form. The same principle applies to painting boats of all kinds—just learn to draw the big, basic shape before you consider the details (Figure 15). First, sketch the basic shape of the hull and lightly indicate the center line from bow to stern. This center line is important, because if a mast or any other part of the boat is off center, the boat won't appear balanced. And a boat must be evenly balanced if it's to stay upright.

It's even more important to sketch the constructions of large boats accurately than it is to capture those of smaller skiffs. Don't concern yourself with the small details. Concentrate on proportions, positions, and perspective—the three "p's." For instance, notice just where the masts are in relation to the hull, how far the foremast is from the bow, and how far apart the two masts are. If the boat is carrying a dory, as most New England fishing boats do, compare the dory carefully to other parts of the boat to determine the correct size relationship.

I don't pretend to know as much about boats as Edmund J. Fitzgerald (Jim to his friends), the author of *Marine Painting in Watercolor*. He's been to sea and he still sails. However, I think the boats I paint would float, and that's more than I can say for some of the boats I see in my students' pictures. Some of them don't understand the construction of boats and won't spend the time required to learn the basic form. The most common error they make is to give the boat a twisted appearance because they don't realize the center of the stern must be opposite the center of the bow. Observe carefully as you draw—and think.

Working Around Boatyards

When a boat is up on land for repairs, the whole boat is visible—what's below the waterline as well as what's above it. Then, too, you can see all the strange junk around the boatyard—rusty oildrums, planks of all sizes, wooden cradles that hold the boats upright, coils of rope, and steel cables. They're all wonderful to draw. In the smaller harbors, where small craft and lobster boats are hoisted onto the wharves for repairs, there's no problem in sketching provided you don't get underfoot. Everything's in the open there and can easily be seen. In shipyards where the big boats are repaired, however, you may have a problem seeing them. They're usually kept behind a high wire fence with a guard at the gate. If you're determined, you may be able to work out something with the repair company. Drop into the boatyard office and ask if you can go into the yard to sketch the boats.

Sketching Boats in Drybrush

I sketch boats in ink, using the drybrush technique (Figure 17). Here's my procedure. First, I lightly sketch the subject with an HB pencil. I use the paper in my sketchbook, which is medium-rough in texture. This pencil drawing is merely an outline, with no textures or tonal values indicated at this stage.

To ink in the boat, I use waterproof drawing ink and old, well-worn watercolor brushes. I dip a brush into the ink bottle, then brush off the surplus ink on a scrap of cardboard and use the half-dry brush on the drawing. I drag the brush lightly across the paper so that it deposits a thin layer of ink on the rough areas and skips the smooth spaces between.

I find that by pressing the bristles down on the cardboard, I can make them fan out to create a fine tool for suggesting grass, weeds, and even wood grain. You can really punish an old brush without feeling bad about it, and there's no end to the variety of textures that can be created with old, almost worn-out brushes. It takes a little experimentation, that's all.

Drybrush is an excellent sketching technique. The materials are easy to carry. All you need is a bottle of ink, a pencil, a couple of old brushes, and a sketchbook. When it dries, the ink drawing is permanent, doesn't need to be fixed, and can't be smeared or blotted.

Don't Trust Your Memory

I've noticed that on completing a shore scene or a landscape with a lake in it, many amateur artists decide to put in a boat—and then proceed to do so without a second thought. The fact that they know nothing about boats doesn't faze them. So I'll tell you now: don't think you can make up a boat or draw and paint one from memory. Unless you know a lot about boats, you won't be able to draw one correctly. So draw or sketch from the actual boat or use good reference material. Don't guess or trust your memory alone.

Fishnets and Lines

Fishermen often hang their nets from the masts of their boats to dry them. These not only make a nice pattern, they also give the artist an opportunity to show off his fancy brushwork. But don't let yourself get carried away. Use broad, simple, drybrush strokes with watercolor, or scumbling with a flat brush if you're using oil or acrylic.

And don't worry about getting all the lines (ropes) in the picture. You need do that only if you're a marine specialist painting to please yachtsmen or professional sailors. Sargent could rig a sailboat with a few quick flips of the brush, and Winslow Homer—who probably knew more about boats than Sargent—was also satisfied with an understatement.

Understanding Reflections

Artists are always interested in the reflections of boats in the water. There are mathematical explanations and diagrams that give the "why's" and "wherefore's" of such reflections, but they aren't really necessary for the outdoor painter. Just remember that the angle of incidence always equals the angle of reflection. This

Figure 16. I did this sketch in Stonington, Maine. There's a lot to see and draw when a boat is out of the water for repairs. In smaller areas such as this, you can easily get close enough to sketch the boat and the objects around it.

Figure 17. I used drybrush for this sketch of a lobster boat with covered cabin and stay sail.

Figure 18. This is a lobster boat in Rockport Harbor. Notice that the reflection of the boat is shorter than the boat itself. I was looking at the boat from a bit higher than water level, and the reflection therefore appeared foreshortened.

Figure 19. Where there are fishermen and fish, there are cats!

means that if you're looking at the boat from the water level, the reflection of the boat on the water will be as long as the actual boat is high, from the waterline to its topmost parts. The reflection of the boat will be exactly the same size as the actual area of the boat reflected. If your point of view is above the waterline, the reflection will be shorter than the actual height of the boat because it will appear foreshortened to you (Figure 18). This principle applies as well to houses, trees, and any other objects found at the water's edge. If the water is still, the boat will have an upside-down, mirror-like reflection. If there's some movement in the water, the reflections will be broken up and will wriggle as the water moves.

Painting Reflections

Now, what about the color of reflections? As I said in Chapter Three, reflections aren't all blue. The reflection of a white boat in the sunlight on calm water is very close to white. The sky and the water in the harbor also contribute color to the reflection, so it's safe to say the boat's reflection is usually slightly darker than the boat itself. If the water is muddy or dirty, as most harbor water is, the reflections are correspondingly darker. On the other hand, the reflection of a dark boat may very well be lighter than the boat itself, as the sky adds lighter colors to it. If you train yourself carefully and correctly, you can go ahead and paint and what you do will be close enough to the right color.

Clipper Ships

Now, a word on painting full-rigged clipper ships. They're very popular subjects and are sometimes painted by fine craftsmen who know how to place each sail correctly and put each rope where it belongs. However, these ship paintings have the same appeal as the pictures being made by the so-called "cowboy" artists who paint a West that no longer exists. It's a nostalgic appeal, with a story-telling quality. I'd call these pictures illustrations, a form of commercial art. If I wanted to own a painting of a clipper ship—and could afford it—I'd try to find one painted by an artist of that period. Failing that, I'd do without it. It seems to me it would make more sense to own something by Fitz Hugh Lane, who lived and painted ships in Gloucester a hundred years ago, than to settle for something done in a New York studio from old prints and photographs in 1973.

King Street. Oil on gesso panel, 9″ x 12″. Until a few years ago, I think every artist interested in New England street scenes painted this one when visiting Rockport. But the tall elms are gone now, and the subject isn't nearly as interesting without them, although parts of the street are still good subject matter. I worked there with my Painting Holiday group last year. In fact, the building on the right is part of the famous Peg Leg Motel that was our head-quarters. Students, notice how simply I've suggested the figures. I rendered them in the same spirit and with the same feeling that I did the rest of the sketch. So many students and amateur artists paint the street broadly, then tighten up on the figures and make a separate project of each one. Try to capture the proportions and the action—forget the detail.

7 Streets That Go Down to the Sea

The streets that run down to the sea in coastal towns and villages provide great subject matter for amateur and professional artists alike. They're esiecially interesting in New England towns—Nantucket with its memories of the great whaling days, and Rockport, Massachusetts, with lobster boats on one side of T Wharf and pleasure boats on the other.

The streets of many European villages are so picturesque they verge on being pretty, and that's a quality I'd rather not see in a painting. I still cringe when I finish a demonstration for a class and one of its members remarks that what I've done is "pretty." I once did a demonstration on the main street of a Colorado ghost town, and as I put my brushes down a lady said, "That's what I call an honest watercolor." Now there's a remark that would please any artist. Although it happened years ago, I've never forgotten it. I think a painting can be beautiful, but it should never be merely pretty. There's a difference and it's something the beginner should learn early in the game.

Street scenes never seem to go out of fashion. In fact, they've been popular for a very long time. I believe 18th-century British watercolorists were mainly responsible for their popularity. They toured the towns and villages of Europe, seeking picturesque views to paint and sell to wealthy collectors back home. Today, of course, everyone who travels can bring back a pictorial record captured in color photographs. But artists still paint street scenes, as anyone can see on a summer or fall day in Rockport. The streets of that popular coastal town have appeared in many exhibitions, mainly in works by Anthony Thieme, who used luminous oil colors to demonstrate his marvelous command of tonal values, and Ted Kautzky, whose bold watercolor paintings won a number of awards for their creator.

In art colonies along the New England coast, it's possible to set up an easel and work in peace. An artist at work is no novelty to the local folk, although a child or a child-like tourist may stop for a chat. It always seems strange to me that a dentist, businessman, or bricklayer on vacation feels there's nothing wrong with interrupting the artist's work. I'm sure he'd resent it if the artist dropped into his place of business merely to gab.

Painting On and Off Location

You don't have to paint street scenes on location. You can do them from pencil sketches or photographs in the peace and quiet of your studio. Of course you should paint some street scenes on the spot for the value of the experience. I've painted most, but not all, of my street scenes from pencil sketches no larger than a standard postcard.

If you decide to paint your street scene from a photograph, here's some good advice. First, use pencil to make a black and white drawing from the photograph. Avoid using ink or a wash of paint for this or you might be tempted to copy the tonal values of the photograph. Having made a satisfactory drawing in which you've worked out your composition and solved your perspective problem, put the photograph away and paint from the drawing. It takes a bit of will power to do this—to keep from stealing a look at the photo—but if your drawing is a good one and if you really *observed* the scene when you took the photograph, you won't need to look. And the painting will be better for it. It won't have that "done from a photograph" look so prevalent in today's watercolor exhibitions.

Visual Memory

I just mentioned that you should observe your subject matter closely. By that, I mean you should train your visual memory. When you look at a scene, be it a country landscape or a city street, you should not only *observe* it but also *think* about it and remember it. Any veteran landscape painter has a good visual memory. He's been observing and thinking about nature for years. As a demonstration stunt, I've sometimes asked the audience to name a subject—winter landscape, marine painting, street scene, for example—and I've painted the one requested. For a class in Arizona, I once painted Fifth Avenue in New York City. It wasn't as difficult as you might suppose. My visual memory has been very well trained. It was just a matter of doing one of my old street scenes from memory. So, get to work, and *think*!

Simplify

Working from memory always reminds me of something the great American teacher Robert Henri once said: "The beauty of working from memory is that so much is forgotten." Whether they work from nature or from photographs, beginners seem unable to resist the temptation to pile detail upon detail, trying to do what the camera does and do it as well or better. This is especially true when they're painting a street scene because there's so much detail to be seen—windows, doors, doorknobs, picket fences, gates, and shutters.

Well, what's a poor, inexperienced artist to do? First, write the word "simplify" on a piece of paper and stick it to your paintbox where you can see it while you work. I admit that simplification is difficult to learn, but it's not impossible and it creates a much more pleasing picture. You simply have to adopt a professional attitude and get out of that rut, that state of mind in which you think if you copy nature in all its complexity you've made a work of art. You haven't.

Then, study the works of artists who've painted good street scenes. Start with the 19th-century British painters. Turner and Bonington and their contemporaries painted the streets of England and the Continent. The French Impressionists painted Paris and the villages surrounding it. Look at some of the works of Renoir, Monet, Manet, and Pissarro. A little later, there were Van Gogh and Utrillo. These artists all painted street scenes from which we have much to learn. Study them carefully, and above all notice the simplification of detail. Their pictures are quite realistic but none look "photographic" even when painted from photographs.

Try to develop a painter's shorthand that suggests rather than copies the detail found in street subjects. For instance, you can put in the shutters alongside the windows of a New England home with a single brushstroke. There's no need to paint the individual slats. Let your brushwork be as personal as your handwriting. Try to make a personal statement. It's not what you paint but how you paint it that'll make your painting interesting.

The Best Time of Year

I think fall is the best time of year to paint the streets of the East Coast. The foliage turns in October, giving the scene beautiful color that can be seen at no

Penobscot Country. Watercolor on paper, 22″ x 29″. This scene is typical of many Maine inlets at low tide, where you find narrow stretches of water between mud flats, and rocks covered with rockweed and barnacles. I did this painting in my studio from the pencil sketch you see above the picture, for which I used a flat carpenter's pencil. To produce a painting as complete as this from so rough a sketch, the painter needs a good visual memory and lots of experience. (Fortunately, I have both!) The smooth Strathmore paper I used lends itself to the technique of scraping into wet paint with a razor blade, and I used this technique in parts of the foreground to create the light area at the bottom. This painting was awarded the Antoinette Goetz Prize at the American Watercolor Society's 105th Annual exhibition, 1972.

other time. Then, too, the light is warm and mellow. And if you get to work before ten in the morning or after three in the afternoon, you'll find the shadows cast upon the road by the tall trees create a beautiful pattern that's not nearly as interesting at high noon when the sun is directly overhead.

Add Some Figures

Remember to put a figure, or several figures, in your street picture. A street without figures is rare indeed. As I suggested earlier, do them simply, without detail, and keep them fairly small (Figure 20). Don't tighten up and make each one look like a separate project. Use the same technique on figures that you use in the rest of the picture. And think carefully about where to place them. Don't put a figure in the foreground (remember that the foreground shouldn't have much detail). And don't crowd them against the edge of the composition. I think the greatest sin of all is to paint half a figure sticking up from the bottom edge of the picture. Figures placed in that position always seem to be standing in a hole in the ground. Sad to say, I've seen this done by professionals who should have known better.

Learn to draw the basic form of your figures in any position. Once you can do this, you'll have achieved something really worthwhile and you'll know it. You'll have the confidence to drop those happy little people into your paintings with authority. Besides learning the basic form, you should sketch people from life. Carry a small sketchbook and make quick sketches on the street, in the park, in restaurants, or wherever you may be. Go after the action, the gesture. Even a small figure in a street scene demands some drawing ability on the part of the artist. The more you draw, the better you'll draw.

Figure 20. Add some figures to your street scenes, but keep them small and simple. Don't make a separate project of each one.

Gray Day, Rockport. Oil on gesso panel, 9″ x 12″. Rockport again. Well, why not? I suppose I must have painted hundreds of sketches in and around that picturesque town. Since it's an easy drive from Boston, it's overcrowded on summer weekends, and artists would be wise to visit Rockport after Labor Day. When I did this sketch, I was looking out toward the harbor from the park across the street. I included cars in this one because they're always there along the wharves, and the place just wouldn't look right without them. Some artists hate telephone poles, I can take them or leave them. I treat them as I do the cars. If they look as if they really belong, I put them in. Sometimes, they add depth to the composition, as I think they do here.

Marizion Beach. Watercolor on paper, 14½″ x 10½″. I painted this on the new Aquarius paper, which has a fiberglass base. It lies flat without buckling, no matter how saturated it is. This is quite surprising in such a light-weight paper. I'm not sure it'll revolutionize the watercolor paper industry, but I find it interesting to use. Because it contains a small amount of fiberglass, it may irritate sensitive skin. Marizion is a seaside village facing St. Michael's Mount in Cornwall, where the tide goes out a long way and leaves a great stretch of beach that's part sand and part pebbles. I tried to show an area of the beach in the foreground of this sketch. Notice the variety of brushwork used to suggest the detail.

Linear Perspective

Your paintings of street scenes will contain houses, of course. To draw and paint them correctly, you need some knowledge of perspective—not as much as an architect needs, but at least a familiarity with the basic principles. The main rule to remember is that parallel lines appear to converge as they approach the horizon line. For a graphic example of this, look along a length of railroad track. The rails seem to meet in the distance. This elementary principle is all you need. If you want to study perspective in more depth, I'd suggest you read a textbook. I confess to knowing only the fundamentals, which are enough for the landscape painter.

The Nuisance of Cars

The cars that line both sides of village streets in summer are a damn nuisance. The street—lined with tall elms, green and white shuttered houses, and picket fences—is a thing of beauty. But so often the beauty is ruined for me by that double row of rubber-tired mechanical monsters! What to do? Well, I leave them out. My street pictures aren't entirely true, but I'd rather have it that way. The cars and trucks can go into my city scenes where they belong. I don't want them cluttering up my village street. When I do use them, I paint just one or maybe two; I suggest them simply, somewhere in the background.

Your Point of View

Now for your point of view—the spot to paint from. My advice is to paint street scenes from the sidewalk, looking at them from ground level. That's the point of view we see them from most often. I can't stand those "looking-down-views." Excuse the pun but I think they're for the birds.

Abstract Patterns

Try to create a good abstract pattern in your street scene. That is, choose a few big, main shapes and try to arrange them well in your picture space. Do this before you think about details or about what the objects actually are.

I've already discussed the best time of day to paint a street scene, but I should point out that the longer shadows created in early morning and late afternoon are a great help in establishing an abstract pattern. Organize the areas of light and shade and use them as part of your picture composition.

A Cape Ann Beach. Oil on canvas panel, 12″ x 19″. Home-made panels are much more satisfactory than store-bought ones. It's not difficult to make them if you're willing to spend the time. I glue raw linen to Upson board, turn an inch of the material over the edge all around the board, and glue it to the back. I paint the front with two or three coats of acrylic gesso and give the back a coat of latex wall paint to prevent warping. The result is a fine panel, sturdier and with a better working surface than the panels for sale in artist's supply stores. Of course, you can use Masonite instead of Upson board, but it's heavier and more difficult to manipulate. If I intend to use the panels with oil paint, I like to size them to make the surface less absorbent. To do this, I use retouch varnish thinned with turpentine and tinted with some burnt sienna oil paint. I haven't said much about this picture except to tell you what it's painted on. That's important—and what else can I say about all that sand?

In the Sun, La Jolla. Watercolor on paper, 12″ x 9½″. I think I've caught the "feel" of southern California in this watercolor sketch, although I can't explain why that's so. Perhaps it's because the light there is different from that in New England. At least, I hope I've succeeded. A Californian might not agree. I remember how I felt about the paintings a friend from that state did on his first visit to New England. They were familiar "down East" subjects, but with California light and color. I think if you compare this painting to my Eastern beaches and saltmarshes, you'll easily see the difference in the light. When an artist works on location, I feel he should paint an impression of that particular place—of the color and light that exists there—and not carry his ready-made formula for picture-making everywhere he goes. Anyway, it was a lovely, warm September day at La Jolla, where we'd been visiting with Fred and Eileen Whitaker.

Wally's Light. Watercolor on paper, 15″ x 20″. Actually, this is Greens Ledge Light in Long Island Sound. But Walter D. Richards of New Canaan, Connecticut, has painted it so often—in all weathers, from all angles, and at every time of day—that his artist friends have christened it Wally's Light. When Wally comes to the monthly meeting of the Fairfield Watercolor Group with another lighthouse painting or lithograph, there's always a lot of good-natured kidding about it. I thought it would be fun to paint his favorite subject and present it at a meeting. I was sure it would get a laugh—and it did. The painting is straight watercolor, done as rapidly and as directly as possible. I used tissues to blot and soften the edges of the clouds.

8 Who Can Resist a Lighthouse?

Lighthouses have great appeal for artists, especially artists from the inland states—we coastal dwellers are inclined to take them for granted and probably don't paint them as often as we should. The average person may think that lighthouses are all alike, but this isn't so. Like people, each lighthouse has its own character. There are tall ones and short ones, some very plain and others all "gussied up" with red and white stripes, some round, and others square. I've never seen one that wasn't interesting, and most of them make good painting subjects. There's one on Long Island Sound that artist Walter D. Richards has painted from all angles and in all types of weather. In fact, he's painted that lighthouse so often that his artist friends call it "Wally's Light."

I suppose the best-known and probably the best American painting of a lighthouse is Edward Hopper's *Two Lights*. Andrew Wyeth also used lighthouses as subjects, but the ones I've seen were painted in watercolor and lack the majesty of Hopper's large oil. I painted my first lighthouse picture, *Two Lights on Cape Elizabeth, Maine*, many years ago, and perhaps because it was also the subject of Edward Hopper's greatest painting, it threw me. I've painted better, much better pictures of lighthouses since then, but I never painted that one again. I feel that once a great artist paints a particular subject, it's better to let it alone. A million to one, no new painting will be any better—so why do one at all?

However, there are hundreds of lighthouses along the coast that haven't been immortalized yet. So, what are you waiting for?

References and Common Sense

I've never understood why many amateur artists who live far from the ocean paint subject matter they're unfamiliar with, such as ships and lighthouses. Some of the boats they draw would never float, and they place the lighthouses so close to the edge of the rocks that they seem to be in danger of being washed away by the very next storm.

If you have a burning desire to paint marine subjects, even though you may live in Tulsa, Oklahoma, it's not up to me to make rules that forbid you to do it. But, if you're going to paint ships, lighthouses, or anything else you know very little about, I'd advise you to do a bit of research about it in your local library before you begin. Get some reference material such as photographs, illustrations, or old prints that will at least give you some idea of the character and construction of what you intend to portray. Professional illustrators, who are often asked to paint pictures of subjects they've never seen, become familiar with their subject matter this way.

It's all a matter of using common sense. You wouldn't expect a native of a fishing village in Maine to paint a grain elevator in a landscape that would satisfy a Kansas farmer. So, whether you paint ships or seas or sealing wax, don't be lazy. And above all, don't think your imagination alone will be enough to carry you through. However . . .

And Then the Ocean. Oil on gesso panel, 9½″ x 11″. It would probably take a psychiatrist to explain why I paint so many lighthouses without showing any ocean. I don't know. They just seem to look best that way. It was the foreground of wonderful weeds that first attracted me, then I saw that crazy catwalk leading up to the lighthouse. I'd never seen one like that before and I just had to capture it for my lighthouse collection. (Just like the man with the butterfly net!) There was a fog coming in from the ocean and it had just reached the lighthouse. I finished the whole foreground in my studio from memory. The fog blotted out the world.

Hendrick's Light. Watercolor on paper, 9½″ x 11½″. Here's another lighthouse picture with no ocean in sight! I wonder why! It could be that I'm heeding the advice I so often give to students when I tell them to avoid painting the obvious. What's the obvious way to paint a lighthouse? Perched on a rocky headland with surf splashing around its base. In this painting, I carefully considered the picture space, the area within the four borders, as space to be designed in an abstract pattern. I used some opaque white in the color washes—not enough to make this an opaque watercolor, but just enough to create the lighting effect of that particular day. I liked the contrasts in tonal value between the lighthouse and the sky. Seen from the other side, with the sun coming from in front instead of behind, the values would be reversed. The main part of the tower would appear light against a darker sky. Remember, correct values create the illusion of reality. Collection Mr. and Mrs. Milton George.

Use Your Imagination, Too

Combined with common sense, imagination is a handy thing to have. I'll give you three examples of how I used the little imagination I have to paint lighthouse subjects. First, I once painted the lightkeeper's house and ignored the lighthouse attached to it. That lighthouse is located at Eastern Point at the entrance to Gloucester harbor, and if you've ever been there you'll appreciate what a great piece of ignoring that was! On the other hand, of course, you may think it was a mistake. The second example of using imagination is a painting I did showing only the upper half of a lighthouse, viewed against a foggy sky from across a weedy field, with no rocks or ocean in sight. I had to take liberties with the actual terrain to create this one, but it did make an unusual lighthouse picture.

The third example is my painting entitled *The Lightkeeper's Daughter*. The young girl is the focal point of the picture and there's no lighthouse, just a rocky garden in which she's gathering some late fall flowers, with a stand of northern pines in the background.

Where to Put the Lighthouse

What a musician does with combinations of notes and a writer does with words, the painter does with shapes and tonal values. It's the arrangement of the main shapes within the borders of the canvas or paper that make or break the picture. You should give serious thought to the composition of any picture, and especially to that of a lighthouse picture. Consider each shape carefully before you think about details.

The lighthouse itself will probably be your picture's main point of interest. Therefore, you shouldn't place it directly in the center of the canvas or it will divide the space in half vertically. Your composition must have unity—that is, all the elements must appear to belong—so be sure that the size of the lighthouse is correct in relation to the other elements. Don't make it too large for the space or so small that it looks like a toy. And remember that you don't have to include the entire lighthouse. A part of it will say "lighthouse" just as well and, in fact, it may make a more unusual picture. Andrew Wyeth painted a watercolor close-up of a lighthouse window. And, as I said, I did one of a lightkeeper's house and left out the lighthouse it was attached to!

Drawing Lighthouses

Draw carefully when you begin a painting of a lighthouse—it's no place to be sloppy. Paint as freely as you like, but do it a sound drawing.

Most lighthouses have rounded tops, and you should use ellipses to establish their form and character. As you draw, you'll no doubt be looking *up* at the lamp and the deck or gallery running around the deck. You should be particularly careful to draw the curve of the ellipses correctly from this angle. When the ellipse is above your eye level, remember that the side nearest you will appear to be curving *upward*. It's surprising how many students fail to observe this point and treat the ellipses as if they were below the eye level. Figure 22 illustrates how the ellipses should be drawn on the entire lighthouse when the top is above eye level.

Making Lighthouses Look Round

A student once asked me how to make a lighthouse look round. Because the tall lighthouse was a dazzling white against the blue sky, she was unable to see the

Figure 21. This is a sketch of the little lighthouse at Cape Spencer, New Brunswick. I place the lighthouse to the right of the center, to avoid dividing the picture space in half.

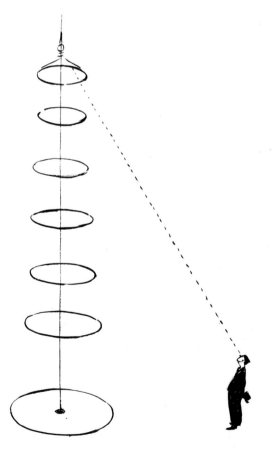

Figure 22. When you draw rounded structures, think in terms of ellipses and remember that they appear flatter as they rise above eye level, rounder below.

October. (Left) Oil on gesso panel, 16″ x 20″. This is my favorite month in Maine or in any of the New England states. It's in October that the rich, warm colors of the marsh grass, weeds, and bushes make such a delightful contrast against the cool tones of the distant headlands and the ocean. In this painting, notice how the warm color of the foreground advances and the cool color of the distance seems to recede. Also note the change in tonal value from the nearest headland to the farthest one. It's this change from warm to cool color and from dark to light value that suggests depth and establishes perspective. The strong light on the water gave me an opportunity to paint the wharf almost in silhouette.

Dragger Close-up. (Above) Watercolor on paper, 8″ x 11″. A walk along the wharves of Gloucester or any other commercial fishing port presents the artist with all manner of subject matter—boats with all their complex gear that's so mysterious to the landsman, ropes, winches, cables, pulleys, nets, radar, and much more. How is it, then, that the average artist repeats the same old dockside composition that's been done and done and done? It usually consists of two fishing boats tied side by side to the dock, with bows toward the viewer, casting long, wiggly reflections in the water. It's because it's been done so often that the subject has climbed close to the top of the cornball list. Oh, I've been guilty, too. That's why I searched for another way to paint this Gloucester fishing boat. This is it—a variety of shapes and colors with almost abstract qualities, yet quite realistic. So, students, think before you paint those fishing boats. Don't be a repeater. The subject provides material for a good painting. Why not make it unusual as well?

Figure 23. This is the Longships Lighthouse off Land's End, Cornwall, England, that Turner painted in his *Land's End*.

subtle change of value from the lightest light to the slightly darker tone on the shadowed side. Keep in mind that the part of the lighthouse facing the source of light is the lightest and that the form becomes darker as it turns away from the light. To create the illusion of reality, it's simply a matter of observing tonal values correctly.

Painting the Beam of Light

The beam of light that sweeps out from the lighthouse at night creates problems for beginners. The main mistake they make is to paint it with such sharp edges that it looks like a piece of yellow cardboard pasted on the night sky. Like sunsets, I think it's best not to paint the light at all. But if you want to paint it and you can't see the real thing, go to the nearest airport, where you'll probably be able to see a searchlight sending its beam skyward. Observe the beam carefully and note that its edges aren't sharp, but soft and diffused.

If you're using oil paints, you can blend the edge of the light beam into the dark tone of the sky with a dry, soft brush. With watercolor, you'll have to blend the dark sky into the light. To do this, first paint the beam of light, then moisten it with clean water and use your brush to draw the dark tone of the sky up to the light while the paper is still wet.

Melodramatic Pictures

As I said earlier, I hope you won't be tempted to paint the beam of light. Such pictures always seem melodramatic to me. They remind me of those paintings done on black velvet which, I'm sorry to say, can still be seen in places catering to tourists.

Perhaps my aversion to what I think are ghastly productions began with one that hung in my grandmother's house in England. Some seafaring relative had brought it home. Its title was *The Bay of Naples with Vesuvius in Eruption.* The artist had really outdone himself. He'd painted flames shooting up from the mountain's cone like the biggest Fourth of July setpiece you ever saw. Then there was white hot lava falling on the sailing vessels in the bay, as well as little figures jumping from the ships into the water. All this was painted on a black velvet background. Is it any wonder I grew up detesting this type of art? That is, if by some stretch of the imagination you can call it art!

I tell that story to impress on the beginner that there's no need to be melodramatic, no need to tell a story in the picture. Leave that to writers and to Norman Rockwell, who can do it very well indeed. As 19th-century English landscape painter John Constable once said, "There is room for a natural painter." And there still is. So, take your paints and brushes into the fields and along the shore and try to make a simple statement of what you see and how you feel about it. Don't try to improve on nature or force her to tell a story. If you're honest with yourself and love nature, that'll be enough.

A Corner of the Marsh. Acrylic on gesso panel, 9″ x 12″. I found this interesting tangle of weeds and rushes in a corner of a marsh just a short walk from the busy Westport railroad station. I'd gone there to paint the saltmarsh with its distant view of Long Island across the water. I don't spend a long time looking for subject matter. When something as good as this presents itself, I sit right down and paint it. (I sat on the ground to do this one.) You just have to know what makes a picture when you see it. Acrylic is a good choice of medium for this kind of close-up. Because it dries rapidly, it's possible to work up a lot of detail in acrylic without having as much build-up and mess as you might with oil paints, and without waiting through the drying periods watercolor requires. I painted most of the sharply defined details with pointed, soft-haired watercolor brushes.

Wild Chicory. Acrylic on cardboard, 16″ x 20″. In late summer and early fall, this beautiful plant flourishes along the coast near my home. It doesn't last long when it's picked, so, as I do with most close-ups, I painted this subject where it was growing. I did this painting as a demonstration for an outdoor class. I remember telling them that close-up means exactly that—*close up*. So many artists, when they first attempt this type of subject, take in too much. It's important to create the feeling of being there among the plants or whatever else you've chosen as the subject of your close-up. I first scrubbed background tones over the entire surface, using a sponge and an old, worn, house-painting brush to apply raw sienna, yellow ochre, burnt sienna, burnt umber, and Thalo blue. I mixed the blue with raw sienna for some green tones. The flowers were the next to go in, and then the stems and leaves, all of which I painted in with brushes. I made the fine light lines with a small, pointed water-color brush.

Salvage. Watercolor on illustration board, 10″ x 14″. This is one of a series of paintings I made of the wreck of the Sea Prince on the coast near Gloucester. Opportunities to paint such a subject don't occur very often. I made several sketches and took some photographs of the wreckage. In this sketch, the ship is completely broken up and men are busy salvaging the gear that can still be saved. It was a wonderful tangle, making beautiful designs over and between the rocks. The color, which doesn't show here (more's the pity), was also dramatic. Bright red machine or engine parts and pale yellow pieces of wood and planks contrasted against the dark green and brown seaweed-covered rocks. I wish now that I'd made this picture larger—maybe one day I will do a larger one.

9 *Beach Debris: Driftwood, Shells, and Seaweed*

There are many subjects to paint all along the beach, not only in summer when bathing beauties distribute their disrobed bodies on the hot sands, but also in the autumn months when high tides and storms leave all manner of debris that the artist can use. After Labor Day, the beaches usually aren't kept clean and tidy and the work force doesn't seem to care if a wandering painter steps on a broken bottle or has to plod through mounds of seaweed! A lot of debris accumulates before the winter's over, and it's not removed until the spring. During fall and winter, the beach is not only the beachcomber's delight, it's also a painter's paradise. The debris doesn't have the same appeal as a bikini-clad cutie, but it's very interesting in its own way.

Close-up Pictures

A close-up picture is one in which one or just a few objects are the entire subject and are painted at fairly close range. Remember that "close-up" means exactly that: *close up.* Beginners often have the desire to do this kind of picture but include too much of the surrounding area, so that the very subjects that attracted them become dwarfed and unimportant. Standing up at an easel won't do you any good here. Get down on your knees or sit on the sand. You've got to be close to the subject. Andrew Wyeth sketched the fragile blossoms of the woodland wild flowers for his *Spring Beauties* while lying prone on his stomach. Even so, he evidently wasn't satisfied with it. The catalog of the exhibition in which this lovely painting appeared mentions that he cut the picture down at the top—no doubt to make it more "close-up."

Painting Close-ups

When I do a close-up study in oil paints, I place my 12″ x 16″ paintbox on the ground alongside of what I'm about to paint. I place a panel in the slots of the open lid and paint on it in that position, using the lid as an easel. After taking out brushes, palette knife, rags, and paints, I place my palette back in the box and proceed to paint. I forgot to mention that I sit on the ground while I do this!

For acrylic painting, I use the same method except that I set a water jar beside me on the ground. When I do a close-up painting in watercolor, I carry a 16″ x 20″ piece of Masonite, to which I fasten a quarter-sheet of watercolor paper with masking tape. I place the old green canvas envelope that held the board on the ground, take my painting gear from my knapsack, and place it on the envelope. I find a rock or piece of wood to lean the board against, and I'm ready to paint.

That's my working method for close-ups. With experience, you'll no doubt find ways of your own. However you paint them, these close-ups are great fun. But remember, they must be done *close up.*

Paint as Found—Don't Rearrange

After Labor Day, objects that can be used in close-up paintings often litter beaches, making them look quite different than they are in July and August. The happy hunting ground for these objects is the high-water mark (the highest point the tide reaches on the beach), or even higher if there have been big storms to blow the debris around. When you're looking for objects of this kind, the thing *not* to do is to collect them and take what you find back to your studio. It's tempting to arrange the material indoors, but if you do all you'll have is another still life in studio lighting. To me, a group of objects tastefully arranged on a tabletop with that same old fishnet background is never as interesting as the same objects tumbled together by nature on the beach.

I think the best approach is to *paint these subjects as found*, right there on the spot. Of course, you should consider your point of view carefully to arrive at the best composition possible. By using the objects as found, you'll paint a picture with a feeling that no conventional still life ever has, in the brilliant light of the great outdoors.

Mixing Grays for Driftwood

What color is driftwood? Most people think it's silver-gray. That's close—it does have that bleached-out look that could be called light or silver-gray. But don't be too ready to accept this as gospel. The closer you study a piece of driftwood, the greater the variety of subtle color you're likely to find in it. Its color really depends on what kind of wood it is. Not all pieces of driftwood were once part of trees. There's also wood from boats, buildings, and if the beach is near a fishing port or harbor, from some broken parts of lobster traps and other fishing gear.

It's no great problem to mix grays in oil or acrylic if you stop thinking of gray as a mixture of black and white paint. Think of gray as a color. There are cool grays and warm grays. To make them, simply mix warm and cool colors with white. The more warm color you add to the white, the warmer the gray; the more cool color—you guessed it—the cooler the gray. With oil paint, I use loose mixtures of cadmium orange, cerulean blue, and white for my grays. You can also substitute burnt sienna or burnt umber for the cadmium orange and try other blues such as ultramarine and Thalo. It's all a matter of using warm and cool colors with white, instead of that old standby black. You can use all the above colors except cadmium orange when you're working in acrylics. Acrylic cadmium orange seems to produce tones that are more green than gray.

The white paint can't be used at all in traditional, transparent watercolor. It's opaque and makes mixtures with other transparent colors opaque, too. However, watercolor paper itself is white and you can create gray tones by allowing the white paper to show through your washes. Payne's gray is a popular watercolor pigment that's convenient and highly valued by some painters. I no longer carry it in my outdoor kit, but I sometimes use it when working in my studio. On location, I prefer to mix warm and cool gray tones from Thalo blue and burnt umber or cerulean blue and burnt sienna. Then, there are the beautiful tones known as "palette grays." I'm not kidding. These are the grays made from paint left on the palette. Painters also call it "palette mud" and some of them do use it for gray tones.

The Color of Shells, Sand, and Seaweed

The beach isn't just gray. There are also the rich greens and browns of seaweed and the blue tones of clam shells. There are patches of sand and a variety of

Hazy Morning. Opaque watercolor on paper, 15″ x 18″. I first covered the entire surface of the paper with opaque white paint tinted with some yellow ochre watercolor. This undercoat blended to some extent with the colors I painted over it. In sky and water, I used light tones of pink and blue. The jetty is a warm gray. The rocks below it are a gray-green, as is the beach along the water's edge. Because this was an industrial area, the foreground rocks were covered with oil and slime and were quite warm in color. That was helpful, because they contrasted against the cool color in the distance to create a feeling of depth.

October Morning. Oil on gesso panel, 16″ x 20″. I painted this on a bright, breezy day at Reid State Park. The park is located on one of those long "peninsulas" that reach out into the Atlantic along the Maine coast. Actually, although they look like peninsulas, many of them are islands joined to the mainland by bridges or causeways. A glance at a map of New England will be enough to show you that the Maine coast is made up of a mass of islands of all shapes and sizes. Better yet, get a copy of the decorative historical map painted by artist Ruth Rhoads Lepper of West Southport, Maine, and you'll readily see why this small area, with all its variety, is so rewarding to the artist. Reid State Park is on Georgetown Island, which was permanently settled in 1624–26. If you go to the park to paint it, you'd better go after Labor Day. It's a state park with miles of beautiful sandy beach, and that means there are always crowds of people there on a sunny day. In October, you'll have the place to yourself as I did.

pebbles and rocks. If you add raw sienna to the oil, acrylic, and watercolor palettes I described in *Materials and Tools*, you should have no difficulty in handling all the colors you find on the beach. In spring and fall the colors are mostly gray, anyway.

Above my desk hangs a beach watercolor, *The Sandpipers*, by New England artist Don Stone. This beautiful painting, one of my treasured possessions, is all done in tones of gray, from the pale, almost white sky to the deep, green-brown gray of the cast-up seaweed in the foreground. The time of the year is early spring or late fall, when the beach is strewn with debris. A broad band of seaweed mixed with pebbles, sand, and shells leads the eye to a young woman dressed in white, seated on the sand watching some birds. Some scrubby bushes and the roof of a house appear against the sky in the distance. There isn't a bright color anywhere in the picture, and it's beautiful.

Collecting and Exploring

When I say you should paint beach close-ups as found, I don't mean you should never collect the treasures. It's fun for the inlander to take home some salty maritime souvenirs: I can recall one young lady who picked up a beat-up lobster float on a Cape Ann beach and carried it back to California.

I think fall is the best time of year to roam the beaches—from the water's edge up over the shingle, through the seaweed and over the rocks, right up to the woods and marshes. A short walk like this sometimes yields enough material for a couple of still life pictures. Any non-painters who see you pick up what to them is junk will think you're a nut, but they already think that about artists, anyway. So why worry!

The Other Side. Watercolor on paper, 7½″ x 10″. Yes, it's a strange title, but it won't sound so strange to you when you know the circumstances! I'm sure every student, amateur, and professional artist in America is well acquainted with Andrew Wyeth's famous painting *Christina's World.* I painted this sketch in the same field that he used in his painting. If Christina Olsen had looked away from the house instead of toward it, this is the view she would have seen. Every artist who has the opportunity should visit the Olsen House in Cushing, Maine, which is now a Wyeth museum. It contains a fine collection of Wyeth drawings and watercolors. This watercolor is a sketch, a "quickie," painted for a group of students who were traveling with me on a painting holiday. I liked the color of the warm-toned autumn grass that contrasted against the dark green pines and the distant blue hills. Collection of Mr. and Mrs. Tony van Hasselt.

10 Coastal Vegetation

The painter who works along the coast usually becomes so excited about the ocean, surf, rocks, boats, and harbors that he gives scant attention to another source of subject material close at hand. It's the coastal vegetation I'm speaking of, and it's always right there underfoot. If a painter sees it at all, it's with a passing glance, a casual look. He may murmur "pretty" to himself and hurry down to the rocks, lured by the sound of the pounding surf or memories of pictures by Homer and Waugh. Little does he know he's just passed up some great material. The plants and wildflowers on the grassy slopes, among the rocks above high water, and along the edge of the woods present a great opportunity to any artist interested in painting close-up pictures. The vegetation changes each season of the year, and it's best in spring and fall.

Quaker Ladies

These charming little wildflowers, also called bluets and innocence, can easily be described as dainty and petite. They flourish on the East Coast and into the Midwest, although I've only seen and painted them in New England. In late spring and up to midsummer, the headland at Rockport, Massachusetts, is covered with thick clusters of these delightful little pale blue flowers. I once painted my wife Elsie gathering a Quaker Lady plant to transplant into our lawn. I guess I owe my interest in wildflowers to Elsie, who's something of a nut on the subject. When we travel on painting trips, there's always a bouquet of assorted wild plants and flowers in our motel room, gathered by Mrs. P. in the surrounding countryside. Oh yes—the bluets she transplanted survived and come up on time every May.

Seaside Goldenrod

There are about 135 species of goldenrod in this country, but my favorite is the seaside variety. My picture of it is reproduced on p. 42, and I hope you enjoy looking at it as much as I enjoyed painting it on a lovely fall day at Deer Isle, Maine. This variety of goldenrod is seldom as tall and slender as those growing inland, and it has chunkier blossoms. It's a sturdy, tough plant—as it has to be to survive living so near the ocean. Its deep yellow is a superb contrast to the violet blossom of the New England aster, which flowers at the same time of year. In the demonstration on page 140, I'll deal fully with the wild aster and say all that needs to be said on how to use it as a painting subject. And I'll leave it to you to seek out other possibilities for close-up wildflower compositions. I'm sure there are many more than I've mentioned.

Trees Along the Coast

What would landscape painting be without trees? Trees have color and design. Some have dignity while others are twisted or dwarfed. A tree heavy with

Figure 24. These are the Torrey pines found along the California coast.

Figure 25. In Maine, the pines sometimes grow so close to the ocean that they seem to be growing out of the rocks.

summer foliage can be a beautiful sight; the same tree in winter when its leaves have fallen can be just as beautiful.

There are trees worth painting on both United States coasts. The varieties of trees found on each coast are wonderfully different from one another. The Northeast has trees that put on a "big show" every fall staging what could be called a color spectacular. California has trees found nowhere else in the world—for instance, the torrey pine found along the coast just north of San Diego. It has clusters of long gray-green needles on many-branched, contorted limbs. Figure 24 is a drybrush drawing of this interesting tree, which I sketched in Torrey Pines State Park.

Artists long ago discovered the picturesque possibilities of the Monterey Cypress near Carmel. In fact, the little grove at Cypress Point has just about become the Motif 1 of the West Coast. (Motif 1 in Rockport, Massachusetts, has become one of the most often painted wharves on the East Coast.)

Trees are also a very definite part of the Maine landscape as they march down the headlands to the sea. The evergreens seem to outnumber all the others—fir, pine, spruce, and hemlock are plentiful. Many are so close to the water's edge they appear to be growing out of the rocks. Before the turn of the century, a Maine doctor's daughter, Sarah Orne Jewett, wrote a book that's become an American classic. Its title is *The Country of the Pointed Firs*. I never see or paint the trees in Maine without picturing that girl riding in the buggy with her father when he made his calls up and down the coast.

Try to learn a little about the different species of trees, if only so you'll know that they're not really all alike, not all Christmas trees. I'm afraid we take trees for granted. It's when we start to draw and paint them that we discover how little we know about something we grew up with. Even a city-dweller sees trees, but he never really *observes* them.

The Colors of Summer Foliage

Mixing the colors of foliage sometimes presents a problem for the amateur artist. In the summer, my students complain that everything is green, and that's true up to a point. Of course, leaves are green in summer, but there's an infinite variety of greens found on different trees. I think those who complain depend too much on the prepared greens of their tube colors, and that's a mistake. Once an artist learns to mix greens on his palette, those ready-made greens will probably disappear from his paintbox, as they have from mine.

Green is a mixture of blue and yellow. However, there are many blues and many yellows to choose from, and each new combination creates a different green. In all three media—oil, acrylic, and watercolor—raw sienna is a fine yellow to use in mixing greens. With Thalo blue, it makes a beautiful, deep, rich green. With cerulean blue, it makes still another green. You can also use a cadmium yellow with a variety of blues, although I've found that gamboge is better than cadmium yellow in watercolor mixtures. You can't buy greens like these ready-made in tubes.

Northern Pines and Autumn Foliage

The pine trees on either coast are beautiful, but I know the ones in the Northeast best. I've learned to paint them broadly. It's just as pointless to attempt a rendering of individual pine needles as it is to try painting every leaf on an elm or maple. The northern pine, with its deep, rich green creates a fine contrast against the deciduous trees (those shed their leaves) when they change color in the fall. In October, a dark green, close-growing band of pines with a blaze of scarlet maples

Cornwall's Connemara. Acrylic on gesso panel, 15″ x 25″. This name was given to this stretch of coastal moorland by W. H. Hudson, who roamed its paths searching out its bird and plant life. He is best known as the author of *Green Mansions*, but his book *The Land's End* is, in my opinion, still the best one written about this bleak but beautiful part of the Cornish coast. Great rocks dot the landscape, their gray granite bulk encrusted with lichens of many colors. It's a very ancient land. I painted this acrylic from a watercolor sketch and a photograph. I tried to render as much detail as possible without making the picture tiresome or destroying its unity. I worked directly on the white gesso ground, using large, soft-haired watercolor brushes to lay in the composition, then switching to the smaller sizes to render the details.

Penobscot Country, No. 2. Oil on gesso panel, 24″ x 42″. When I do a good painting, I'm often curious to see how the same subject would look painted in a different medium. I've often based oil paintings on my watercolor paintings and vice versa. However, the two paintings are never exactly alike, as you can easily see by comparing this oil to the watercolor version on page 77. I've included a smaller area of sky here, and I've placed greater emphasis on the light-struck water. Though still simple in treatment, I feel the design of the foreground has been improved in this version. There's a more effective lead-in from the bottom right corner up over the rocks to the tall tree against the sky. The headland behind the tree now directs the eye back to the right. The round rock and the reflections of trees on the right bring the viewer's eye back down to where it started. I used copal painting medium and a limited palette to paint this picture—yellow ochre, raw sienna, burnt umber, burnt sienna, cerulean blue, Thalo blue, and white.

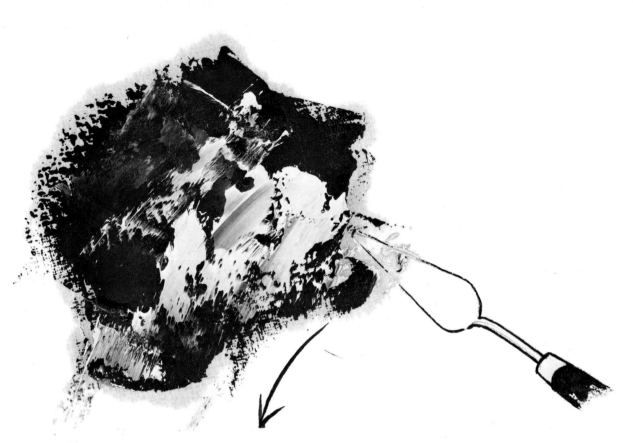

Figure 26. When I paint large masses of trees, I often begin by applying the darker foliage color. Then I add the lighter colors with a painting knife. The arrow here indicates the direction in which I move the knife as I apply the paint.

Figure 27. To create grass textures in watercolor, I often use my fingernail to scratch out wet paint. This technique is especially effective on smooth paper, because the paint sits on the surface and can easily be removed.

in front of it is a beautiful thing to see. I think I can describe it with paint far better than I can with words.

Painting Trees

How do I paint pine and maple trees I've just described? Well, here's one way. I first paint the dark pines, using one of the green mixtures I've suggested. I use a painting knife to apply the color of the scarlet maple over the dark green, holding the knife flat against the canvas and using a dragging stroke (Figure 26). This is one of my favorite methods of rendering foliage, because I can easily create interesting textures with a painting knife. It's a useful tool, but guard against overusing it. If you use a knife throughout a painting, the trees are all apt to look alike and the picture will be merely an exhibition of technique. I think a combination of knife and brushwork is best, especially when you're painting large masses of foliage where you need a variety of textures.

When you're painting trees, don't make a separate project of each tree. In other words, don't finish one tree at a time. Paint the foliage mass as a light and dark pattern, an abstract arrangement, then merely suggest some detail. I always put in the branches and trunks last, placing them where they'll do my composition the most good. You can also scratch in dead branches or twigs with the point of a painting knife, but that's another trick that shouldn't be overdone.

I've seen beginners paint green balls on sticks to represent trees. After they've had some experience, they sometimes improve, but all their trees still look alike. They scrub in masses of green paint and add some branches and a trunk without giving any thought to what kind of tree they're painting. Trees have character. No two are exactly alike. When you paint trees into a landscape, observe them carefully and think about what they are.

Grass Textures

There are usually areas of grass in coastal paintings. Sometimes it's just ordinary grass on the headlands or slopes between the beach and the woods. It may also be the marsh grass called salt hay (which I'll describe in more detail in the following chapter) or that coarse grass found on the sand dunes. Like tree foliage, grass should first be indicated as a tonal mass, then the detail merely suggested. It's a mistake to start painting individual blades of grass with a small brush. In watercolor, I often use my fingernail to scratch details into the wet paint in the grass areas (Figure 27). When I'm working with oil paints, I use a brush handle or the point of a knife.

Saugatuck Shores. Oil on gesso panel, 20″ x 28″. This is on Long Island Sound near my home in Norwalk, Connecticut. I'm fond of using marshes, especially saltmarshes, as subject matter. Although marsh pictures don't seem to be very popular with the general public, I think they're great. And I'm sure that John Constable would have been as thrilled as I was the morning I saw this one for the first time. I like the shape of the big mass of trees on the right and the way the mass is balanced by the small tree on the left. A glimpse of the water and a suggestion of beach cottages in the distance add depth to the composition. I pre-toned the white gesso panel with a mixture of white and raw umber oil paint thinned with turpentine. I painted the entire picture with thick, rich pigment, making my brushstrokes follow the forms, as you can readily see in the foreground.

11 Saltmarshes Along the Coast

For readers who live inland, I should explain that a saltmarsh is a low-lying area along the shore that's almost completely flooded by the ocean at high tide. Fresh water streams also flow into it, cutting channels, forming ponds, and creating a brackish mixture of salt and fresh water. A coarse grass grows on the highest parts of the marsh. Called salt hay, it's green in summer and in the fall its color runs from pink through all the shades of ochre and orange.

There may be salt marshes along the Pacific coast, but I didn't see any when I was in California. However, there certainly are plenty of them up and down the Eastern Seaboard. Tall, dark pines form a background for the saltmarshes along the northern Atlantic coast. The breathtaking contrast between the low marshes and the pines has a great appeal for me. I think it's one of the most beautiful subjects found along any coast.

Some artists think marshes are nothing special to paint, and there are many picture buyers who feel the same way about them. I remember years ago, my old friend Ulysses Ricci of Rockport told me, "Marsh pictures don't sell." But he introduced me to the marshes on Cape Ann, and since then I've tried to paint them every fall when I visit that beautiful part of the New England coast.

The fact that the picture-buying public doesn't appreciate marshes surprises me, but I think I know the reason. The unsophisticated buyer who's out to acquire a picture for his livingroom thinks first in terms of subject matter. To him, a marsh makes an empty picture. If the painting contains a picturesque, broken-down barn or a couple of hunters all set to slaughter some innocent ducks, it's more of a picture to him. Sky and marsh alone aren't enough for such buyers. But the person who does buy a marsh painting buys it for a number of reasons. He may want a good painting by an artist whose work he especially likes. He may admire the technique, the way a particular picture's been painted. Or perhaps the color scheme or composition attracts him. This man doesn't think about subject. He likes art. The other one needs educaiion.

Composing an Open Marsh Painting

What about composing your marsh painting? After all, composition is a matter of good taste, and I don't think I should lay down any hard and fast rules about it. However, it won't do any harm if I restate a few of the popular notions that artists and teachers have on the subject.

First, the shapes in a marsh picture consist mainly of horizontal areas of land, water, and sky. You should be careful to avoid a monotonous arrangement of horizontal lines and shapes that lead the viewer's eye in a straight line from one side of the painting to the other. Use curving lines and design your shapes so that they lead the eye *into* the composition. These elements, along with the use of warm and cool colors, will give your picture the illusion of depth.

Another principle of composition is the warning not to divide the picture space exactly in half—either horizontally or vertically. This is good advice, be-

Ipswitch Marsh. Watercolor on illustration board, 22″ x 30″. I'm very fond of this place and have painted several pictures there. It was the late Harrison Cady, the man who drew Peter Rabbit for so many years, who first took me there. This is the view across the marsh to the creek and Labor In Vain Bridge. How's that for a name? I wonder what circumstances led to the naming of the bridge, and who did name it. I took full advantage of the illustration board when I painted this. Notice the brushwork in the large tree. It wouldn't have been possible to create such texture on a rough surface or on pre-soaked paper. To make the scratches that helped develop the character of the salt hay in the foreground, I ran my fingernail along in the wet paint. This, too, was no problem on the smooth, hard surface.

Along the Coast. Watercolor on paper, 7½″ x 10″. I've nothing much to say about this small sketch, except that I painted it from memory when I was preparing to go out to do a demonstration. My usual practice is to carefully plan my demonstration subject in sketches like this, take it to where I'm performing, then forget to look at it. This sketch is a composite of many of the Maine coastal subjects I've painted, and I suppose it grew out of my memories of them. There are two paintings in my *Oil Painting Outdoors* that are very much like this.

cause a landscape in which the horizon divides the sky and the land into equal parts is rather dull. You should try to avoid this especially in a marsh painting, in which the value patterns—marsh and sky, dark and light—are very simple. I suggest you compose your painting to include either more sky than marsh, or vice versa, to add interest by making the two value areas unequal in size. To do this, you must either place the horizon line below the center of the picture for more sky area or above the center for more marsh. As a rule, I let nature dictate the choice for me. If the sky is beautiful on a particular day, I feature the sky and its interesting cloud pattern. If the sky is blank, on the other hand, I place my horizon line high on the canvas and feature the marsh itself.

I'm sure everyone who has the urge to paint also has an instinct for design. However, I'd like to point out that your marsh paintings and other landscape subjects will be better if they're more realistic than decorative, even though you may have to simplify some of the complexities of nature to achieve such a result. I constantly preach *simplification* to my students, and I never feel it's necessary to take stylish liberties with nature.

Point of Interest

You've probably heard the statement, "Every picture must have a center of interest." This is, one area or object that's more important than the other elements in the picture. I prefer to call it the *point* of interest because the word "center" leads beginners to believe it should be placed exactly in the middle of the canvas—which, of course, isn't true. In fact, the picture is more exciting if you don't place it in the center!

Wherever you place your point of interest, remember to design the other shapes in the painting so that they lead the eye directly to it. You can do this even with a simple subject like a marsh or landscape. The point of interest doesn't have to be an unusual object. It can be a simple shape or a tonal value, such as that created by a dark group of trees placed against a light sky or the reflections of the sun in a tidal pool.

Colors to Use for Marshes

If you decide to paint marshes, these are the oil paint colors I suggest you have in your kit: cadmium yellow light, yellow ochre, raw sienna, burnt sienna, cadmium orange, English red, burnt umber, Thalo blue, cerulean blue, and alizarin crimson. The only difference between this oil palette and one used for watercolor is the substitution of a light red watercolor paint for English red. Winsor & Newton's watercolor light red is about the same color as English red in oil. You may have noticed that I haven't included any green pigments. As I said earlier, I prefer to mix my greens from combinations of yellows and blues.

In the fall, I find raw sienna the most useful color in painting marshes. It mixes well with yellow ochre and alizarin crimson to create the rich, warm tones needed for the marsh grasses in the foreground. When you introduce the cooler blues into the distant parts of your picture, you'll create an illusion of recession or depth. (Do I need to remind you that cool colors appear to recede and warm colors seem to come forward?)

A saltmarsh is the ideal place to use warm and cool colors this way, because nature has already arranged the landscape accordingly. In autumn, the foreground grass displays a lovely variety of warm colors, while on a clear day the distant ocean may be pure cerulean blue. And if you look in the direction opposite the sea,

Saltwater Farm. Watercolor on paper, 15″ x 20″. On the Maine coast, one comes across small farms that consist of a few acres and are quite often partly composed of marshland. I've heard these called saltwater farms, and some of them are owned by men who divide their time between farming and lobstering. (On a coast where lobsters abound, why not?). This is a bold, spontaneous watercolor. It demonstrates an approach I think all watercolorists should try to master when working directly from nature. I wasted no time fussing with finicky details. Notice the simple three-value rendering of the house and of the rust-streaked tin roof of the long shed that's reflecting the light. Note also how simply I've handled the weeds and grass in the foreground. An overworked foreground would have competed with the point of interest—the buildings and the pond below the bank.

Gathering Rushes. Watercolor on paper. I used opaque watercolor and white paint
throughout this painting. I first painted the surface of the paper with white toned with a
little yellow ochre. Then I painted the colors over this undertone and allowed them to blend
into it. I put the final darks in when everything else was dry. These include the darkest parts
of the figures and the fallen branch in the foreground. I created textural interest in the tall
rushes by scratching the paint with my fingernail and a brush handle. Painting onto a white
undertone is an old technique and can yield interesting results. It works well for painting
foggy subjects on the coast. Try it—you'll like it!

chances are you'll see a distant hill or some pine trees. These also need cool color to make them appear distant.

Texturing Marsh Grass

You don't need texture in the distant parts of your painting, but foreground grasses or salt hay do need some textural interest. When I'm working in watercolor, I use my fingernail to scratch suggestions of grass and weeds into the damp paint (Figure 16). Remember, I said *damp* paint. If the paper's too wet, you'll scuff the surface and cause the paint to run into the scratch, making a dark line instead of a light one. With oil paints, I paint the light tone of the grass over a darker underpainting, using a small, pointed, sable watercolor brush. I keep a few sables with my oil brushes because once they've been used for oil they can't be used with watercolor paints.

Capturing the Feeling of Light

Marshes are flat surfaces under open sky. They're therefore full of light, and you should try to capture this feeling of luminosity if you want your statement about the marsh to ring true. Watch even the shadows—they have a great deal of reflected light in them and they're very colorful. You won't find any black or very dark tones in the shadows. Black is the absence of light, and light is everywhere on a marsh, especially a saltmarsh near the ocean. I can't imagine a marsh painting without light and atmosphere!

The mood of the day is also very important to me. I want the viewer to *feel* the weather in my picture, to know what kind of day it was when I painted it. What's the sense of going to nature to paint if this isn't the goal? I might as well design wallpaper!

Lifting Fog. Watercolor on paper, 15" x 20". I painted this in late September—a good month to work on Cape Ann. The summer crowds have departed by then, and the weather is still warm enough to make being out along the shore a pleasure. New Englanders say the fog is "burning off" when it lifts and that's the correct expression, because the heat of the sun actually does make the moisture evaporate. Except for the warm color of the marsh grass on which the old lobster boat rests, most of the colors here are cool gray tones. Notice the closer values—the strong note at the water's edge is the only large dark. Also study the bold big-brush treatment I used to suggest reflections and movement in the foreground water. It's this kind of spontaneity that makes a watercolor "sing." To see spontaneity at its best, look at the watercolors of John Singer Sargent.

12 Sky, Clouds, and Atmosphere

"It is a strange thing how little in general people know about the sky. It is the part of creation in which nature has done more for the sake of pleasing man, more for the sole and evident purpose of talking to him and teaching him, than in any other of her works, and it is just the part in which we least attend to her."—John Ruskin

It's true. The average person doesn't pay much attention to the sky. We walk up the road or drive along the highway and don't consider the sky unless we're wondering if it's going to rain or snow. A glance serves to tell us the day will be gray or sunny, and that's that. Even today's artists seem to ignore the sky. How many paintings do you see nowadays in which the sky occupies the major part of the canvas or paper? Very few, and I wonder why.

Up to fifty years ago, landscape painters were still interested in painting a sky picture now and then. I remember the works of some of the painters who were approaching old age when I was a young student. There was Charles H. Davis, who lived in southern Connecticut and painted skies that equal anything the great 19th-century English painters did. I admired him greatly. And there were others whose names are forgotten now. I was pleased when I recently discovered a fine color reproduction of a Davis painting in *The American Impressionists*, by Donelson F. Hoopes. I think there are signs of a new interest in natural landscape paintings that don't distort or render nature as a collection of fashionable tricks. This transition seems to be taking place on the East, if not on the West, Coast.

The Sky Isn't Flat

I've tried to impress upon my students the beauty and importance of the sky for the landscape painter. They say, "But skies are so hard to paint." Fiddlesticks! It's not more difficult to paint skies and cloud formations than it is to paint anything else. Could you play a violin concerto after a few lessons? Good painting isn't easy—you have to work at it. The first thing to remember when you're painting the sky is that it's not a flat backdrop, not a sheet hung up behind the landscape. The sky has depth. It extends beyond the horizon. Look at the clouds and you'll see that they diminish in size as they get farther away from us.

What are Clouds?

Clouds are made up of tiny particles of water and ice crystals. They also may contain dust particles, especially when they're over cities, which give clouds color by reflecting light. Clouds over cities and industrial areas differ greatly in color from those over areas where the atmosphere isn't polluted. There are also layers of dust and smog between us and the clouds. At sunset, the low angle of the light makes the dust visible and the clouds are then at their most colorful.

Painting Clouds

Painting clouds has to be memory work—you can't change your painting as the cloud formations change. When you're painting moving cloud formations, rapidly sketch the overall pattern with a pencil, a brush, or charcoal. Then paint from memory, except for an occasional glance at the color of the sky.

When I work outdoors, I always paint the sky area first. I usually paint the big cloud shapes, using a mixture of white and a little yellow ochre. The large cumulus clouds, whose light areas look so white, often appear to have a pale yellow edge where they meet and contrast against the blue of the sky. I use a little yellow ochre instead of a more intense cadmium yellow for these edges. I add the blue areas of the sky next, then deal with the areas of the clouds in shadow.

I often paint the shadow areas of clouds with grays made by mixing cadmium orange, cerulean blue, and white. If I'm working in watercolor, I mix a gray wash from a warm and a cool color, such as burnt umber and Thalo blue. I go easy on the blue because Thalo has great tinting power. Of course, I use several other combinations, too, depending on the type of clouds I'm painting, the time of day, and the weather. I sometimes use a red, light red, or even alizarin crimson with one of the blues, and I find it useful to mix ultramarine or cobalt blue with red.

While I'm doing this, I keep in mind the advice Sir Joshua Reynolds gave a fellow artist. He said, "Let your clouds' shadows be of silver, not of lead."

Creating the Effects of Atmosphere

Creating the effects of atmosphere in a landscape is important. But how do you do it? First, study the tonal values carefully. As you compare one value to another, you'll notice that they all appear higher as they recede into the distance. (Under certain weather conditions, this doesn't happen, but on a clear day along the coast or in the country, values do become higher toward the horizon.) Also, the distant parts of a landscape appear cooler in color—you know, "beyond the blue horizon." If you use warm tones in the foreground and cool color in the distance, you'll create a feeling of depth, an illusion of atmosphere.

You can also suggest the effect of atmosphere by simplifying your painting. Overworking the details not only destroys the unity of a landscape but also kills its feeling of atmosphere. I often warn students against taking a still-life approach to nature—that is, filling the whole painting space with detail so that the viewer reads the picture inch by inch. We don't take in nature that way! I know there are people who love that finicky type of technique. But in my opinion, it's better suited to *genre* painting than to the kind of landscape painting we're concerned with here.

Many of those who admire the detail of Andrew Wyeth's egg tempera paintings don't realize that his power as a designer, not his ability to render detail, makes his paintings good. Painting minute details isn't as difficult as the nonpainter might suppose. With time, patience, and a good photograph to work from, or a willingness to sit outdoors in front of the subject day after day, any good craftsman can render detail. However, if you lack the ability to organize the composition, to design it so that if all the detail were eliminated the picture would be a fine abstract, the time you spend noodling the detail will be wasted.

Examples of Atmospheric Effects

There are certain places where you can easily see the effects of atmosphere. A mountain top is one such spot. There, you can look for miles and see range after

Foggy Morning. Watercolor on paper, 8″ x 14″. This is a quick note, a sketch, which I set down before the fog burned off completely. I painted it on Bristol board, which has a very smooth surface and was a good choice under the existing weather conditions. Washes dry rapidly on smooth paper because there's no grain to trap and hold the water. Anyone who paints watercolors in the fog along the coast will appreciate this.

Offshore Lobsterman. Oil on gesso panel, 9″ x 12″. I painted this spontaneous little oil sketch on the shore within the town limits of Rockport, Massachusetts. It was a gray day, with plenty of moisture in the air. The lobsterman hauling and baiting his traps close to shore attracted me as a painting subject. Later, I became so interested in painting the rocks and beach that when I was ready to put him in the painting, I found he'd gone. No matter, the distant boat was so small that it presented no problem. Although I designed the beach with rocks on the left and right in order to lead the viewer's eye to the boat, it's the beach itself that's the point of interest. The advantage of working on these small panels is that you can paint a lot of them on your one- or two-week vacation.

Land's End, Cornwall. Watercolor on paper, 14″ x 20″. Turner sketched these massive cliffs from the same viewpoint I used in this picture. The picture painted from his sketch is one of the world's watercolor masterpieces. I carried my sketchbook to Land's End the last time I visited Cornwall, and I painted this picture from a sketch when I returned home. No doubt my use of dramatic lighting was influenced by memories of Turner's great picture. I used a smooth Bristol board and did quite a lot of work with my razor blade on the rocks. It's worth the effort to experiment with smooth paper. Some artists like it, others think it's simply awful. I have one artist friend who scorns its use but freely uses Maskoid on every watercolor he paints! I painted this watercolor using a very limited palette—just yellow ochre, burnt umber, and Payne's gray.

Wanderlust. Oil on cardboard, 10″ x 14″. I was working at what I expected to be a rock study, nothing more, when young Jon appeared and stood gazing out to sea, at a ship on the horizon. The opportunity was too good to miss, so into the picture he went. I also carried out my original intention of painting the rocks with only a painting knife. The day was bright and clear, as it often is on Cape Ann in October.

range of mountains disappear into the haze. There's so much atmosphere between you and the farthest range that although you know it's as rugged as the closer ones, you don't see any detail on its face.

Near St. Ives in Cornwall, where Frederick Waugh painted his fine early seascapes, there's a place along the cliffs called Five Points. From there, it's possible to see five great headlands thrusting out into the Atlantic. The details of the nearest one are easy to see. But because of the intervening atmosphere, the details of the others become less distinct until there's no detail visible at all in the farthest point.

Such atmospheric effects are present in all landscapes and seascapes. The two examples I've just mentioned are more obvious than some, because these areas contain large receding land masses.

The Color of Rain

There are plenty of atmospheric effects to observe on a rainy day. Contrasts in color aren't as strong as they are on a bright day, but there are visible differences in tonal value. I've seen good rainy-day scenes painted in only three colors. You can paint a watercolor rain scene using only burnt umber, yellow ochre, and Payne's gray. In oil, use the first two colors and mix ultramarine blue with ivory black to make a color that resembles Payne's gray. (Payne's gray is a mixture, not a pure color, that some manufacturers have started putting in tubes for oil painters. It's easy to duplicate it with other colors on your palette.)

Painting Rain

The old-time artists loved to paint distant showers. The artists of the Hudson River School made great use of them, and so did those hardy souls who went West to paint the first pictures of the Rocky Mountains and the canyons.

The painter of the coast can often see the same effects as he looks out to sea. When a cloud on the horizon drops rain, a gray shadow seems to extend from the base of the cloud to the ocean. It almost seems that someone put a wide, flat brush into the cloud and pulled some of it down into the ocean at an angle. And that's the way to paint it—rapidly, simply, and broadly. Use the largest flat brush you can handle confortably and make downward strokes from the clouds to Mother Earth.

Near Two Lights, Maine. Oil on watercolor paper, 16″ x 20″. This is another of the marine paintings I did on my first trip to Maine thirty years ago. What an exciting summer that was! We stayed with Phil and Marion Yates, a painter and a musician from Philadelphia, in a cabin so old a rock was working its way upward through the livingroom floor. Philip Yates was one of my teachers and a great man. Not only was he a landscape painter, but he was also a fine wood carver. He'd carved frames for Robert Henri, Edward Redfield, N.C. Wyeth, and other artists who were active at that time. It was great fun to get up early, have breakfast, then drive down to Cape Elizabeth or up to Bailey's, stopping on the way to gab with fellow painters from New York, Philadelphia, and points west. Then we made the rush to the rocks, selected a spot, and began the morning's work. Here, you see the result of one of those mornings many years ago. I painted this directly and haven't touched it since.

13 The Camera: Its Uses and Misuses

Many, very many, of today's painters work from photographs. This is nothing new. Artists have been doing it for a long time. But it's strange that almost to a man they seem to think there's a stigma attached to the practice, as though it's something to be hidden, a skeleton in the closet like the idiot aunt in the attic. Perhaps they think if they keep quiet about it, no one will suspect. The general public may not, but their professional brothers aren't fooled one bit.

This attitude is doubly strange since, in recent years, it's been widely publicized that world-famous artists use photographs. Van Deren Coke's recent book, *The Painter and the Photograph*, discusses the use of photographs by such famous artists as Delacroix, Manet, Degas, Gauguin, Toulouse Lautrec, Edvard Munch, Ben Shahn, Cézanne, and Picasso. The American realist painter Thomas Eakins also used photographs—Gordon Hendricks make it the subject of his book, *The Photographs of Thomas Eakins*. Vuillard, the French painter of those delightful interiors, was an enthusiastic amateur photographer who used photographs to paint his family and artist friends.

Does that shake you up a bit? It shouldn't, because when the camera is used intelligently it can be a useful tool. Go back over the list of names I've mentioned and then try to picture the work of some of these artists. Not one could be called a "photographic painting," with the possible exception of Thomas Eakins' and his paintings aren't as photographic as you might suppose.

Before photography was invented, the old masters tried all kinds of tricks. In *An Introduction to Dutch Art*, by R. H. Wilenski, there's a chapter on "Vermeer's Mirrors" and a description of how other Dutch artists of that period used mechanical contrivances to assist them in painting their pictures. Girardot used reducing glasses through which he saw the model in reduced scale. Then why do our present-day painters make such a fuss about not using the camera? Most of them do use it anyway, and I'm certain the old masters would have, too, if that little black box had been invented in their day.

Color or Black and White?

If you're going to use photographs as a reference in painting, I think it's best that you use black and white film. I advise this because color film isn't perfect. It seldom reproduces the actual colors found in nature. The blues are always too blue and the reds too hot. It does a much better job on a gray day, when there isn't as much color to photograph. Color film doesn't do well on duplicating the tonal value range, either. Unless the photo is taken by a good, professional photographer, the shadows in a sunny-day landscape are bound to be too dark.

I think you'd be better off with a black and white photograph and some notes about the colors you see. That way, you won't be taking the chance of becoming a "photo copy-cat." Remember, those artists I mentioned earlier didn't have color photographs to work from at all. If you must work from color shots, watch out for those false tonal values and the too-intense color. There's no point in doing what the photograph has already done, especially when it's already been done *wrong!*

Top of the Dune. Watercolor on paper, 15″ x 22″. I painted this on a misty morning at Good Harbor beach, as a demonstration for my class. The beach and the seaward view were so fogged in that the dunes were the only visible subject. To get away from the usual, done-to-death sand dune picture, I asked my wife Elsie to pose—which was no surprise to her! Against the sky, knee-deep in the dune grass, she started picking weeds—which didn't surprise me! In fact, I'd counted on it. It furnished a reason for her presence in the picture. Notice the wet-in-wet treatment in the dune grass and the final drybrush touches, added when the paper had dried to suggest individual blades of grass and shadows on the sand. The figure is almost a silhouette in its simplicity. That—simplification—was the whole point of the lesson, during which I repeated my command many times to "keep it simple."

The Sadie Noonan. Acrylic on gesso panel, 12″ x 16″. I came across this famous old Glouces-ter schooner tied up on Rocky Neck, where it was being re-fitted or rigged or whatever the correct term is—not so that it could go to sea and fish the Grand Banks again, but so that it could be placed in an exhibit at a maritime museum. There, for a price, the general public can now go aboard the schooner, walk the deck, and go below to exclaim over the cramped quarters the crew lived in at sea. This painting is an acrylic "quickie." In it, I tried to simpl-ify the complexity of detail one always finds around ships and boatyards. That fine painter of boats and harbors, the late Gordon Grant, had a summer studio near this place. Perhaps he also saw the Sadie Noonan. I've been told it was quite a wreck before it was brought here for a face-lifting.

Merlin's Cave. Watercolor on paper, 12″ x 14″. King Arthur's castle at Tintagel on the coast of Cornwall has been in ruins since the middle of the 16th century, but to visit it is to feel at once on hallowed ground. It's the ancient land over which Tristram and Iseult once walked hand in hand. At the base of the cliff directly below the castle is Merlin's cave. I painted the rock face of the cliff on smooth, 2-ply Bristol paper, using burnt umber and making it rather opaque by adding very little water. Then I scraped the dark paint with the edge of a razor blade, using it like a squeegee. The rock textures emerged almost magically. If you wish to pursue it, you might find that this technique can lead to interesting and unique results. For me, it was simply an experiment. On second thought, the procedure is too tricky—forget it!

Composing From a Photograph

One thing to keep in mind when you're composing a picture from a photo is the fact that you don't have to accept the photograph "as is." When you use the camera to photograph landscapes in nature, it usually takes in too much of the view. Such panoramas aren't often painted today. Study your photograph carefully before you begin. Perhaps by cropping off some of the left, right, top, or bottom, you can find a composition within it that's better than the whole. Then block out the unwanted portion with a piece of masking tape.

Take Your Own Photographs

Some amateurs think that if they copy a photograph from a magazine or newspaper, they'll produce an original work to which they can attach their signatures. Not so! The professional who took the magazine photo was the originator and solved the problem of selection and composition himself. There's also a danger in exhibiting such a painting. Someone else may have seen the photo it was copied from and broadcast the information. This could be most embarrassing. I remember a watercolor that won a prize in a major exhibition. A fellow artist discovered it had been copied from a photograph in an old *Life Magazine*. So, amateur artists, take your own photographs. It's the only sensible thing to do!

Refresh Your Memory—Don't Copy

There are places where it's not possible to set up your easel—the center of a city street or along the coast during a hurricane, for instance. These places offer great pictorial possibilities, so why not use your camera? You don't have to use it as a crutch. Just use it as a reference to refresh your memory, and don't allow it to take over and dominate your thinking.

When you work from a photograph, just remember it's important not to copy. Don't get trapped into copying the tonal values in the photo. They're probably false anyway, because no camera can be entirely accurate. Don't let yourself end up with a skillful copy of a photograph. It would only prove that you're a skillful copyist, not an artist.

Railroad Bridge. Watercolor on paper, 10″ x 15″. When the train leaves Westport, Connecticut, it crosses the Saugatuck River at this point as it continues northeast. This is the mouth of the river, and just beyond the bridge is Long Island Sound. This is another example of a rapidly painted, direct statement, an impression of what has been called "an eyeful of nature." I made no attempt to paint anything but a visual suggestion of what I saw. Holding on to the first impression is the important thing in outdoor painting. The watercolorist uses a kind of shorthand to obtain his effects and should keep simplicity in mind from start to finish. There should be no looking into things to find more and more detail, no making a separate project of each part and thereby destroying the picture's unity.

On the Marsh. Watercolor on paper, 15″ x 22″. This was a stormy day near Reid State Park, Maine. I consider this painting to be a good example of spontaneous watercolor treatment. When the weather is changing quickly, as it was that day, the artist has to make his brush fly. When he does, especially if he's working in watercolor, he often does his best work. It doesn't pay to get too comfortable when painting outdoors! For the grays in this sky, I used a mixture of burnt umber and a little Thalo blue, for the band of dark trees, raw sienna and Thalo blue. The marsh grass was a mixture of raw sienna and burnt sienna, the water, the same colors as the sky. I don't know why I'm telling you this when the picture is reproduced in black and white. Sorry 'bout that!

Derelict. Watercolor on paper, 8″ x 10″. Two abandoned hulks have been "resting" at Wiscasset, Maine, for years. Everyone paints them. I've seen some great work inspired by the remains of these old sailing ships, and also some that was pretty awful. The two hulls are about all that's left of the ships now, but I can remember when they still had masts, some spars, and lots of tattered hanging ropes. I wish I'd had sense enough to paint them then. One was called the "Hesperus"—no kidding!—and I've forgotten the name of the other. To obtain strong, deep darks in watercolor, such as the ones I've used in this sketch, you must have plenty of paint on your brush. Some amateurs use so much water in their washes that their darks dry too light. And then there are those who soak the paper before they start to paint. I think that's also the wrong way to do a watercolor outdoors.

Demonstrations

The following demonstrations are step-by-step reconstructions of seven paintings that I've completed during the past few years. I've chosen to include them here because I think they're representative of the subjects and techniques discussed throughout this book. As you follow the progression from first step to finished painting in each demonstration, I hope you'll think about the wide variety of maritime subjects there are to be painted and see how many ways there are to paint them.

The art student 1923

The instructor 1973

Fishing the Surf: Step 1. Watercolor on paper, 25″ x 19″. I diluted opaque white watercolor paint with water and tinted it with a little yellow ochre. I mixed enough to cover the entire surface of the paper and used a 1″ flat brush to apply it. This wash should be thin enough to allow the pencil drawing to show through. I used Winsor & Newton Chinese white, but you could also use PermaWhite or Poster White.

Fishing the Surf: Step 2. I painted the sky tones into the wet underwash and used Payne's gray for my cool tones. Along the horizon, I put a warm tint of burnt umber mixed with a little cadmium red light. Note the soft edges which I easily obtained by rapidly working into the wet, semi-opaque tone. I set in the shape of the turning wave and the ocean with a pale wash of cerulean blue.

Fishing the Surf: Step 3. I turned my attention to the beach and washed in the lightest tones, using mixtures of Payne's gray, burnt umber, and cerulean blue. Soft, blended tones appear here because I picked up some of the first semi-opaque wash as I applied these tones. The purpose of this step was to develop the big pattern of the beach area. I tried to maintain this pattern or design as the picture progressed.

Fishing the Surf: Step 4. This step was probably the most important one—the one before the final touches were to be put in. I finished the beach, except for the few foreground darks and indicated the figure in two tones, leaving out the final details. I darkened the water, especially the turning wave.

Fishing the Surf, Long Island. For this final picture I used an old technique. I painted it in my studio from an oil sketch done on the spot. This isn't often done nowadays, but it's interesting and worth a try. When I lived on Long Island, I often painted the beaches there. It was marvelous in the fall when the men and women were out fishing the surf. At low tide, when the wet sand and the tidal pools reflected the sky and the fishermen in luminous, pearly tones, the effect was enough to break a painter's heart.

Wild Asters: Step 1. Acrylic on paper, 12¼″ x 9¼″. I made no preliminary drawing for this acrylic painting. I used 300 lb. watercolor paper. Over the entire surface—except the rock in the top left corner—I painted a loose mixture of yellow ochre and raw sienna, scrubbing it on with a ¾″ bristle oil brush. I painted a wash of burnt umber over the rock.

Wild Asters: Step 2. Here, I developed the background. I first designed a light and dark pattern. Still using the same oil brush, I scrubbed in dark and middle tones of yellow ochre, raw sienna, ultramarine blue, and burnt umber. As I worked, I scratched some indications of stems and grass out of the wet paint with my fingernail. When the background was quite dry, I began to paint in the flowers, using undiluted white paint.

Wild Asters. With the white flowers complete, the picture was ready for the final step. I added more stems and grasses, using a small, pointed watercolor brush and mixtures of cadmium yellow and white. I also used yellow ochre and white in some grass areas. I tinted the flowers with a transparent wash of violet and added the yellow centers last. These colorful little flowers grow all over the New England coast in late summer and fall. Although there are 150 species in the United States, they're all usually called New England asters. They vary in color from blue and purple to white. They're a lovely complement to the yellow blossoms of the seaside goldenrod, which bloom at the same times of year.

Wind from the West: Step 1. Watercolor on paper, 8½″ x 11½″. My usual procedure when I paint cloud formations is to first dampen the paper with clean water. (I said *dampen*—never soak it!) For a paper this size I used a 1″ flat brush to apply the water. Then I put in the blue areas of the sky and the first wash on the under sides of the clouds, using cerulean blue. The only poncil drawing I did was in the land area and to help establish the horizon. Notice the soft edges created as the paints ran together on the damp paper. The only color I used here was cerulean blue.

Wind from the West: Step 2. Using a mixture of cerulean blue and cadmium red light, I began to model the clouds by strengthening the areas in shadow. Then I worked on the rocks and ocean. In the rocky area, I first painted a wash of yellow ochre, then blotted it with a tissue to remove the excess water and added the darks. These were a mixture of burnt umber and Thalo blue. I used some raw sienna for the bushes at the right.

Wind from the West. In this final step, I strengthened the blue in the sky. Because the paper was almost dry, some sharp edges occurred along the top of the large cloud formation. I prefer to call the two preceding steps "reconstructions" rather than actual painting steps. To show exactly what happened, I would have had to photograph each stage as I worked. And that would have been difficult because I was working outdoors and had to paint rapidly to capture the effect. Clouds don't stand still. They're in constant motion, and the painter is forced to hold onto his first impression no matter what else happens up there. After the first long look, sky painting is memory painting. Few sky pictures are being painted today, and I think it's a pity. Here is my impression of a breezy day on Cape Ann.

Low Tide, Rockport: Step 1. Oil on gesso panel, 9″ x 12″. I toned the white gesso surface of this panel with a wash of burnt sienna oil paint thinned with turpentine. I sketched the composition directly with a brush, using burnt umber. Because skies change so rapidly, I put in the cloud formation quickly. As the sailboat was about to disappear behind the pier, I swiftly indicated the shape of the sail.

Low Tide, Rockport: Step 2. This step illustrates the lay-in of the whole picture. I made no attempt to finish any one part. My purpose here was to establish the big main shapes and tonal values. I always advise students to think of shapes and values before thinking of objects as objects. I painted the sky with loose mixtures of cerulean blue, cadmium orange, and white. I mixed my greens from raw sienna and Thalo blue, the darkest darks from burnt umber and Thalo blue. The picture was now ready for the final pulling together, as well as for the details that would create an impression of reality.

Low Tide, Rockport. Notice the broken color of the entire foreground in the final painting. I picked up two colors, a warm and a cool, on the brush and laid them down without mixing them too thoroughly. I added only enough detail to make the painting more realistic. Of course, I saw a lot more detail in the subject than I indicated. It's at this stage that the amateur runs into trouble, because he hasn't yet learned the importance of simplification. For instance, he can clearly see the windows and doors of the houses across the harbor, the separate stones of the seawall, and the complex details of the boats. In trying to finish each of these areas in detail, he causes the picture as a whole to lose its feeling of unity, light, and enveloping atmosphere. Each part takes on the look of a separate project. You must keep the idea of simplification in mind—it's of the utmost importance.

Saugatuck Marsh: Step 1. Watercolor on Fabriano paper, 10″ x 14″. I made a brief sketch to indicate the main shapes, then put in light washes to establish the composition. For the sky, I mixed a warm wash of yellow ochre and a touch of cadmium red light. While this was still wet, I brushed some well-diluted Thalo blue into the upper left corner. I used cerulean blue for the distant trees and mixtures of yellow ochre and Thalo blue for the near trees. I added a little burnt sienna to the same mixture and painted in the marsh grass. For the washes on the water, I used mixtures of cerulean blue and cadmium red, and added some burnt umber in the darker areas. I made no attempt to finish any area at this stage.

Saugatuck Marsh: Step 2. Here, you can see the picture beginning to take shape. I painted a second wash over the distant trees, using cerulean blue and a little yellow ochre. In the large tree mass, I used darker mixtures of yellow ochre and Thalo blue. I rapidly wet the marsh grass area on the center right with clean water because it had begun to dry, painted a cool tone of cerulean blue at the top, and strengthened the dark under side with burnt umber, raw sienna, and Thalo blue. For the water pattern, I used another mixture of cerulean blue and cadmium red, but made it thicker this time by using less water to dilute it. Then I was ready for the final, most critical step.

Saugatuck Marsh. This finished picture is typical of the Connecticut shore, where rivers empty into Long Island Sound. I did this demonstration for an outdoor painting class. I painted it rapidly in order to capture the soft, moisture-laden air of the summer morning. Only in this final stage was the paper dry enough to keep the washes from running and blending together. I added the darkest darks in the marsh and water. My memory goes back many years to a night at the Salmagundi Club in New York, when Ted Kautzky remarked that it's the last ten minutes spent on a watercolor painting that count. This entire final step is an example of those last ten minutes.

Gray Day, Shell Beach: Step 1. Oil on canvas mounted on Upson board, 13″ x 20″. I cut a piece of raw Belgian linen 1″ larger than the panel all around. I spread glue, slightly diluted with water, on the surface of the panel and pressed the linen onto it with my hand. Then I turned the panel over and glued the extra inch of linen down on the back. I gave the front two coats of acrylic gesso. When this was dry, I toned the surface with a wash of burnt sienna oil paint well-thinned with turpentine. I rapidly sketched the composition with burnt sienna and burnt umber. Then, following my usual practice, I started with the sky and worked downward to roughly lay in the whole picture.

Gray Day, Shell Beach: Step 2. This is the lay-in. I used a limited palette of five colors—burnt umber, burnt sienna, cadmium orange, cerulean blue, and raw sienna. (I don't count white as a color.) The cool grays in the sky, ocean, and beach were mixtures of cerulean blue and cadmium orange with white. I also brushed in some of the rocks at the base of the cliff with this mixture. For the dark rock forms, I used burnt umber and burnt sienna and added some raw sienna on the top of the cliff. The warm sand tone was the cerulean blue, cadmium orange, and white mixture.

Gray Day, Shell Beach. This reproduction of the finished painting shows how I completed it by adding final touches over the entire surface. Southern California isn't always sunny. It wasn't sunny that February day at La Jolla when I painted this. If it weren't for that strange, eroded cliff, the low-keyed color and gray tonality of this painting might suggest the State of Maine. (Sorry, Californians!) Most outdoor painters are so anxious to get something down on canvas that they don't think enough about composition until it's too late. In this picture, notice that I designed the space by making the headland the point of interest and leading the eye along the beach to it. The rock shapes forming the cliff take the viewer's eye to the left and the patch of light cloud holds the eye within the picture and draws it back to the beach by way of the wave and surf.

Surf at Andrews Point: Step 1. Oil on Upson board, 10″ x 14″. This is a reproduction of the 35mm. color transparency I worked from. If you intend to use photographs as a painting reference, you should take them yourself. I was lucky to find surf at Andrews Point the day I went there to take this one.

Surf at Andrews Point: Step 2. This is actually the first step of the painting. On a panel of Upson board which I'd given two coats of acrylic gesso, I painted a wash of burnt sienna to create a toned ground. With brush and burnt umber, I then drew in the composition. There are rock ledges at the left and right in the photo. Note that I eliminated the one on the left. I felt they were too much the same in importance and would have created a static, fenced-in foreground.

Surf at Andrews Point: Step 3. This is the lay-in of the big, simple color masses. I gave no thought to details at this stage. I painted the sky first with a mixture of cerulean blue, toned down with a little burnt umber and white. Then I darkened this mixture by adding some Thalo blue and painted in the ocean and the dark part of the wave. The light foam is white, to which I added a touch of yellow ochre to relieve the coldness. I blocked in the rocks with burnt sienna, burnt umber, and white.

Surf at Andrews Point: Step 4. I began to build up textures here. I used thick, rich impasto to model the wave, making my brushstrokes follow the form. I also made a start at indicating the action of the foreground water. I added a greater variety of brushwork and color to the rocks. I put in some cool tones at this step to suggest wetness, using cerulean and Thalo blue. Although I used a thick, heavy impasto treatment throughout this painting, I did it only with brushwork, not with a palette knife.

Surf at Andrews Point: The final painting is what is generally called a marine painting, with the breaking wave about to crash on the rocks. I hadn't painted one in years, but I felt this book needed such an example to make it a complete record of maritime landscape painting. I also wanted to demonstrate the use of photographs to the amateur painter. I'm not fond of this particular kind of marine painting. Waiting for that wave to "go boom" is nerve-wracking! I maintain that this is a very specialized field. Why try to be another poor man's Frederick Waugh—aren't there enough of them around already?

Tips, Comments, and Observations

The following are some random thoughts and ideas—others' as well as my own—that I've gathered during my painting experience. I hope you'll find them interesting, and that some of them will help you in your work.

Paint foregrounds broadly. You can't see the flowers at your feet while you're looking at the trees a hundred yards away. Let the center of the scene at eye level be your focal point.

Scrape and wipe your palette clean each time you finish working. A palette containing heaps of dried paint doesn't tell the world you're an artist. It simply says you're lazy.

When you leave a painting location, leave it as you found it. Take the dirty paint rags home and burn them.

If it's hard to unscrew the caps of your paint tubes, try putting a little Vaseline on the threads.

Don't try to be too comfortable when you're painting outdoors. I've done my best work when the bugs were biting.

Some amateurs spend so much time setting up their gear they're too pooped to make much of a painting.

I've met amateur artists who create their own frustrations. Before starting a picture, they say, "I know this is going to be a mess." A real pro says, "This picture is going to be the best thing I ever did." The great teacher Robert Henri advised his students to pretend they were singing or dancing a picture.

In 1890, at the age of 19, the young French artist Maurice Denis wrote: "Remember that before it is a war-horse, a naked woman, or a trumpery anecdote, a painting is a flat surface covered with colors assembled in a certain order."

Years ago, I used to visit the Metropolitan Museum of Art in New York with an elderly artist friend who was fond of making a little joke now and then. When he entered the Rembrandt room, he'd always say: "Let's get through here fast. He spoiled the business."

One day, in a secondhand bookstore, I was lucky enough to find a copy of *Hunt's Talks on Art*, dated 1875. This book should be reprinted. Here are three samples from its pages:

> "Don't despise anything which you have honestly done from nature. There's a sketch, which when I brought it home, seemed only a patch of bright green there, of violet there, and orange here. A year later, I chanced upon it and found that it was an impression from nature: and that's what our sketches ought to be."

A Moment in Maine. Watercolor on paper, 15″ x 22″. The use of smooth paper for watercolor painting isn't new, but there's been a renewed interest in it recently. I painted this picture on Strathmore illustration board, which has a smooth but not slick surface. Compare this to a picture such as *Up from the Beach*, page 39, which was painted on rough paper and you'll readily see the difference. Although the foregound in this painting is much larger and more important than the sky, it was the sky that attracted me to the subject on that October day. It was very pale at the zenith, but there was a fog bank hovering off shore. This made the distant ocean look like a brilliant silver streak. To capture the effect, I left the white paper untouched in the distant area of water. I avoided overworking the grass and weeds in the foreground, so that I could attract and hold the viewer's interest on the water in the background.

"I have disliked pictures so much that I afterwards found were good, that I want to hint to you that you may, some day, want an outlet from the opinions you now hold."

"Elaboration is not beauty, and sandpaper never finished a piece of bad work."

Don't work with the sun shining on your canvas or paper. Itis hard on the eyes and impossible to judge tonal values on that blinding surface.

Stand up when you paint if you can. Step back now and then to view what you've done.

Never hold the brush as you do a pen. Grasp it halfway up the handle and work from the shoulder. Paint a picture, don't *write* a picture.

Oil painters should learn as much as possible about painting mediums. The standard linseed oil and turpentine mixture is safe, but there are others worth trying. Winsor & Newton's Winton Painting Medium, which contains stand oil, is a good one. So is Grumbacher's Copal Painting Medium. There are formulas for mixing mediums in *The Materials of the Artist*, by Max Doerner, and in *The Artist's Handbook*, by Ralph Mayer.

Don't shampoo your watercolor brushes. Wash them in clean water only.

If you submit a painting to a jury and they reject it, don't question the action. If rejections get you all upset, don't send your paintings in the first place. I've had many rejections.

There's a big boom in cowboy art throughout the American West and Southwest. If you can draw and paint a good horse, you're in. These pictures remind me of an old Cockney lady I overheard in a London gallery during an exhibition of works by Sir Alfred Munnings, the famous English painter of horses. "You know," she said to her companion, "I always sez, after you've seen one 'orse paintin', you've seen 'em all."

The serious young artist today is turning to the figure and human values, to the world he observes around him. He isn't going to be satisfied with turning out decorative designs.

"The non-artist is likely to judge art too much upon the score of subject matter or theme, but he should remember that subjects other than pretty can be important also. Art need not always be pleasant, but it should say *something* and say it in an understandable manner." From *Frederic Whitaker*, by Janice Lovoos.

Near Branford. Watercolor on paper, 9″ x 14″. This is typical of hundreds of inlets on the Connecticut shore of Long Island Sound—lush with summer greenery as it is here, spectacular when autumn changes green to gold and all shades of red, often ice-bound in winter. These inlets are a never-ending source of material for artists who live along this part of the coast. The day I painted this was sunny and hot, and the foliage was so heavy that the trunks and branches couldn't be seen. Except for some final strokes to suggest the action of the water, I painted this entire picture using a 1″ flat sable brush on the cold-pressed Fabriano paper. I completed the sketch in half an hour.

Bibliography

Ballinger, Harry R., *Painting Sea and Shore*. New York: Watson-Guptill, 1966.

Craven, Thomas, *Men of Art*. New York: Simon and Schuster, 1931.

Doerner, Max, *Materials of the Artist and Their Use in Painting*. New York: Harcourt Brace Jovanovitch, 1934. London: Hart-Davis, 1969.

Fawcett, Robert, *On the Art of Drawing*. New York: Watson-Guptill, 1958.

Fitzgerald, Edmond J., *Marine Painting in Watercolor*. New York: Watson-Guptill, 1972. London: Pitman Publishing, 1972.

Henri, Robert, *The Art Spirit*. Philadelphia: J. B. Lippincott Co., 1923.

Leslie, C. R., *Memoirs of Constable*. London: Phaidon Press, 1951.

Mayer, Ralph, *Artist's Handbook of Materials and Techniques*. 3rd ed. New York: Viking Pres, 1970. London: Faber & Faber, 1973.

Masters of British Painting, 1800–1950. New York: Museum of Modern Art, 1956.

Seago, Edward, *A Canvas to Cover*. London: Collins, 1947.

Shipp, Horace, *Edward Seago*. London: Collins, 1952.

Smart, Borlase, *Seascape Painting Step-by-Step*. New York: Watson-Guptill, 1969.

Turner: Imagination and Reality. New York: Museum of Modern Art, 1966.

Wilenski, R. H., *An Introduction to Dutch Art*. New York: Frederick A. Stokes Co., 1929.

Index